A Scattering of Seeds

A Scattering of Seeds

THE CREATION OF CANADA

Lindalee Tracey

McArthur & Company
Toronto

Canadian Cataloguing in Publication Data

Tracey, Lindalee, 1957 –
A scattering of seeds : the creation of Canada

Based on a video series with the same title.

ISBN 1-55278-086-4

1. Immigrants – Canada – History. 2. Immigrants – Canada – Biography. 3. Canada – History. I. Title.

FC104.T72 1999 971 C99-931743-1
F1035.A1T72 1999

Composition, Design and Cover by *Michael P. Callaghan*
Typeset at *Moons of Jupiter, Inc.* (Toronto)
Printed in Canada by *Transcontinental Printing* (Quebec)

McArthur & Company
322 King Street West, Suite 402
Toronto, ON, M5V 1J2

10 9 8 7 6 5 4 3 2 1

To the immigrant who comes on dreams
and bears the mirror that reflects us all.
Keep faith—this place is capable of miracles.

Contents

Preface

This is a country, as the author reminds us, that has never been friendly to those strangers who have arrived here from far shores. Each successive wave of immigrants does its best to frustrate the arrival of the next wave, often on the grounds that "they're taking our jobs". I cannot imagine a sillier argument. The truth is, as some of the stories in this book make clear, that immigrants don't take jobs, they *make* them.

Two of the characters in these pages—and they are all characters—were known to me personally: my maternal grandfather, Phillips Thompson, and my neighbour, Martha Purdy Black, MP for the Yukon. Each was an ornament to the nation that adopted them: both have a place in the history books.

But we must not forget the difficulties that the strangers within our gate suffered in the past. The Chinese, who helped build our transcontinental railways, were treated as pariahs, burdened with a head tax, and forbidden to bring their wives to Canada.

The Sikhs were driven from our shores, even though they were British citizens, during the shameful *Komagata Maru* incident in 1914.

Black Americans were denied entrance to Canada during the great pre-war immigration boom because, it was said, they couldn't stand our cold winters, and this at the very time when another black American was on his way to the North Pole with Robert Peary.

The Ukrainians, known as "Galicians" and "Ruthenians" in the early days of the century, were the subject of intense vilification. To John A. Macdonald's son, Hugh, they were "a mongrel race", to the premier of Manitoba, "foreign trash".

Italian immigrants were not wanted here in the early days of the century: to Clifford Sifton they were "undesirable persons". Newcomers from the British Isles were warned in advertisements for jobs that "no Irish need apply".

Jews were excluded from the major professions and, indeed, from Canadian universities by an infamous quota system that everybody knew about and nobody talked about. In the Thirties an entire boatload were sent home to certain death in Hitler's Germany. And we all know, to our shame, how badly Canadian-born citizens of Japanese ancestry were treated during World War Two.

Have we learned anything from this litany of greed and prejudice? Perhaps. At least the son of a despised "Galician" rose to become Governor General of Canada; so, recently, has the child of Chinese immigrants from Hong Kong. If the story of our immigrants has been a tale of hardship and despair it is also an odyssey of hope and triumph. And that is what this book is all about.

Pierre Berton
Kleinburg, Ontario
October 1999

Introduction

So many of our different people's bones have come to rest in this land, so many of their dreams have fertilized a nation. Too often we speak of our history as an homogeneous thing, ancient hands reaching out of Britain and France and jabbing their flags into our flank. As if they were the only ones.

Too often we lean into our history as a study of great men and some women, who, by their very privilege, were predestined to opportunity and greatness. Yes, we know of Simcoe and Champlain, Papineau and Macdonald. Heroes in their own time always have their biographers. But they were not the only ones.

Just after Confederation, the first national census of 1870–71, counted 3,600,000 of us—just over 2,000,000 British, 1,000,000 French and about 136,000 natives. Already there were smaller numbers of German and Irish and a smattering of American blacks, Chinese, Dutch, Italians, Portuguese, Spanish and Swiss. Over the next century, 9,000,000 more people would emigrate to Canada. By 1986 there were over 25,000,000 of us. But it was upon the backs of the first immigrants that a nation emerged.

We were all strangers once, elbowing for a place called home. Colonial immigration laid the early foundations of Canada, and multicultural immigration built on top of it. We were a nation populated reluctantly and in the image of our colonial administrators. Throughout the seventeenth and much of the eighteenth century, European powers dithered about spending money to encourage settlement. The New World was a place of plunder, where the fur trade took precedence over citizenship and where natives were considered either suppliers or hindrances. As profits piled up, immigrants were waved in as a way to protect trade and colonial land claims. It was a recurring pattern in Canadian history—immigration as flesh on the bones of sovereignty. A way to hold back the English, French and Americans. Later, the dilemma was how to keep immigrants from leaving, especially for the richer promises and louder promotions of the United States.

Hordes of immigrants didn't hurry across the sea at first. New France's population at the time of the British Conquest of 1759 was only about 65,000, and its settlement policies were very exclusive. The Jewish financiers who had propped up much of the fur trade from France were themselves forbidden to settle. But the French who did come had the backbreaking task of beginning a nation, and the unenviable luck of having to dodge the stray bullets of colonial wars. Acadians, who were fourth- and fifth-generation Canadian by 1750, were routed from their homes and sent into awful exile because of the suspicions of the English. It was as close to genocide as Canada ever got. Imagine the horror.

For a century after the conquest, the colony bloated up on its "Britishness," engraving its myths, its laws, its name, in English. When thousands of political refugees came tumbling in from the American Revolution, these Scottish and English United Empire Loyalists fortified Canada's ties to England, its Protestant identity and its anti-Americanism. They shaped a British Canada, rather than an English one. In return, Canada gave them free land, establishing a long tradition of assisted immigration and refuge. Black Loyalists were settled, too, though on scruffier land and more tenuous promises. Later they would help defend their new country in the War of 1812, acting on the loyalty that grateful immigrants would express throughout the nation's history.

As the first layer of Canadian identity began to emerge from the generations of native-born, religion was still the dividing line between "us" and "them." When the Irish came staggering out of the great potato famine, they constituted the first huge influx of "foreign" immigrants—Catholics who preferred city work to farming and who challenged British sensibilities by the simple fact of their distinctiveness. Protestant Canada recoiled, but the Irish brought the necessary labour for the burgeoning industrial economy in central Canada and built its canals and bridges. It took them generations to move out of the shadows of religious tyranny and invective.

Later, when thousands of black fugitives sought refuge from American slavery, Canada offered a tentative welcome. Anti-Americanism took on almost evangelical tones, and Canada positioned itself forever as the morally superior nation. And a safe place.

As the country stumbled from under the skirts of Great Britain and became a Dominion, nationhood forced the promise of an intercontinental railway, which itself lured immigrants with the promise of work. Chinese began crossing the Pacific and coalescing around Vancouver.

Canada had kept little watch on its borders during the nineteenth century, and immigrant movement was largely unrestricted. Official policy was mostly concerned with quarantine stations, the responsibilities of transportation companies and keeping out criminals, paupers and the sick. But in 1885, British Columbia lobbied Ottawa to stop Chinese immigration—now that the work was done, the Asians were emphatically unwanted. An act was passed forcing Chinese to pay a head tax. It was the first of a series of measures meant to keep undesirables out. Restrictive policies against the Chinese, Japanese and South Asians continued until the late 1940s, based not on old religious differences, but racial ones. Living inside the skin of an unwanted colour required a special fortitude. The Chinese drifted eastward, to laundries and restaurant work in cities and towns, offering hands and minds to a nation.

As immigrants crowded into central Canada and good land was gobbled up, demand for food and produce, especially hard wheat, coincided with the election of Wilfrid Laurier's government in 1896. The west had to be opened. Canada's minister of the interior, Clifford Sifton, masterminded an immigration plan that encouraged agricultural settlers from beyond the British Isles, Northern Europe and the U.S. Sifton's famous words echoed through the century: "A stalwart peasant in a sheepskin coat, born on the soil, whose forefathers have been farmers for ten generations, and a stout wife and a half-dozen children is good quality."

Aggressive business and railway interests also clamoured for more immigrants, hoping to reap profits from an insatiable world demand for Canadian resources. Sifton listed potential settlers in descending order of preference: British and American farmers, followed by French, Belgians, Dutch, Scandinavians, Swiss, Finns, Russians, Austro-Hungarians, Germans, Ukrainians and Poles. Further down the list were those who were less desirable in both the public and the government's minds: Italians, South Slavs, Greeks and Syrians. At the very bottom came Jews, Asians, gypsies and blacks.

Lured by Sifton's promotional campaign, western-bound settlers arrived in the hundreds of thousands. Icelanders hurried from their volcanoes and set up their own republic in Manitoba; Eastern Europeans raced from poverty, and Jews from Russian pogroms. A lot of Sifton's advertising was sheer bunk, as startled immigrants soon discovered. Homesteaders found themselves dwarfed on the prairies, clearing swampland, fighting grasshoppers and bending into the icy winds of winter. That they clawed out wheat fields, towns and businesses is nothing short of miraculous. Like the Irish before them, many of these "foreign," non-English, non-Protestant immigrants high-tailed it out of rural isolation for city jobs.

Massive and consecutive waves of immigrants filled up the decade between 1903 and 1913. Jews, Italians, Macedonians, Sikhs, Poles and Finns made their way into Montreal, Winnipeg, Toronto, Hamilton and Vancouver, providing cheap labour and skilled craftsmen for factories and construction. Many took on seasonal mining and lumber work. Their strangeness rattled ethnic and religious anxieties previously reserved for the Irish.

Canadians fretted over immigrant ghettoes and whether or not the children, given time, would be integrated. It was tolerable for faceless immigrants to toil in the fields, but quite another thing to have them rub up against decent society in the cities. While some recognized the valuable service of newcomers laying streetcar tracks, sewing in the textile factories and digging sewers, many demanded strict enforcement of immigration regulations and an outright ban along ethnic and racial lines.

Anti-German and anti-foreigner hysteria erupted in Canada during WW I, souring feelings toward all kinds of immigrants. The devastation of the Great Depression that followed put a tourniquet on immigration. Exclusionary immigration policy was implemented and remained unchanged until long after World War II. While Canadian immigrants bled on foreign battlefields for the Dominion, the wives and children of other immigrants were left stranded in their homelands for years, barred from entry, growing separately from their loved ones. Womenless men formed bachelor societies across the nation, their raw hands working the industrial machines while their hearts stalled on postponed intimacy. Imagine the loneliness.

The boom that followed the end of the war pried Canada's doors open to eastern and western European immigration and eventually to the world. Canada emerged as an urban, industrial power, and new immigrants took on the manufacturing and construction sectors, while better-educated immigrants offered their professional skills. As the horror of the war awakened the world's conscience, it was the children of immigrants who pressured the Canadian government for human rights reform. The federal government moved to eliminate racial, religious or ethnic barriers to Canadian immigration.

By the late 1960s, the last remnants of racial discrimination were eliminated from Canadian immigration policy. In 1971, for the first time in Canadian history, the majority of immigrants were of non-European ancestry, a pattern repeated every year since. Seven years later, a new Immigration Act affirmed Canada's commitment to the protection and resettlement of refugees. The Vietnamese boat people were its immediate benefactors.

Canadian immigration history has been compared to a journey through the Bible, beginning in Lamentations and ending in Exodus. The determination of early immigrants is almost incomprehensible today, as is their lack of complaint. Those who burrowed into this place built a country that hadn't existed before, fitting their sensibilities and cultural values into a consensus, into a national character that is both pragmatic and lofty.

Our multicultural immigrant history is scratched inside the steamer chests of our great-great-grandmothers, scribbled on the musty, yellowing papers of ancestors whose true names were misspelled at ports of entry. Here in the cellars and attics of Canada, in the fallen timber of long-lost homesteads, are the whispers of immigrants who arrived in the future and trembled before it. Who found the courage to keep on going because there was no going home again. Whose language, religion, culture often marginalized them for a generation.

It is the tears of immigrants that moisten the railway tracks, whose bones still groan on the land they opened; whose laughter rings out at the sudden surprise of ourselves. We are their children, gulping in the air of Canada. We are them, the imagined self they invented, braiding their language, Gods and dance into something new called Canada.

I write this book because it is in my own blood to do it, me the granddaughter of an Englishwoman, the great-granddaughter of Irish immigrants, the seventh or eighth generation of French and Acadian. I write this because there is something magnificent about the small people who wandered through our history unaccounted for. Who had the gumption and grit to move blindly toward a promise and to keep their disappointments to themselves. They came long before ideas of entitlement, education, equality, welfare, medicare.

It is the small gestures of history, the personal details, that catch my heart and bring me back from my own exile. History for me is working people's hands; their calluses and swollen knuckles scrubbed clean on holy days. It is hands holding books, kneading bread, hammering fence-posts, patting babies, writing letters home, every scratch a testament to effort, every bitten-down nail an apology, every open palm a nervous welcome. I see hands in prayer, in grief, in gestures of humility as they twist inside themselves behind someone's back. They are the hands of immigrants with work to do, the hands of my people and of me. I owe it to their unrecorded efforts to remember—for to forget is to be orphaned by history and exiled from the greater self.

This book celebrates the efforts of early immigrants to establish themselves, and the cold, hard fact of their survival. While recent immigrants to Canada are even more astonishing for their cultural variety and contributing skills, my reach extends only a little beyond World War I. The experience of the early immigrants deserves separate attention from that of later arrivals, simply because of the enormity of getting here first. In the immigrant narrative that is Canada, the first layer of identity was often dug deepest and with the most difficulty.

Here are the personal portraits of immigrants upon whose bones a nation rises. They belong to all of us. This is their story and ours, not a definitive history, but an empathetic one. Listen to their quiet courage. And imagine.

Philippe d'Entremont

Chapter One
Acadian Spirit: Philippe Mius d'Entremont

CANADA AND THE WORLD IN THE 1650S

The shrine of Sainte Anne de Beaupré is founded on the banks of the St. Lawrence.

Explorers Radisson and Groseilliers begin their first westward journey.

Louis XIV forbids the sale of liquor to Indians in New France.

The first organ is imported to Canada.

The land speaks and ghosts walk in Pubnico. It is a village on the southwestern shore of Nova Scotia, at the head end of a fish-shaped place. Pubnico is a long, thin sliver lodged into the edge of sea, lengthened with adjectives—East and West Pubnico. What seems a conceit is really a testament to the impossible fact of its own existence. Whacked by the blunt end of history, the Acadians who cling to this shore shouldn't be here.

This was once an empire's foothold and a bargaining chip for the debts and vanities of kings. It is where European Canada begins. Those long dead days are remembered as if people here had lived them. They will tell you L'acadie was claimed and settled before the founding of Quebec, before the Pilgrims got to Plymouth Rock and the Dutch colonized New Amsterdam on Manhattan Island. In Pubnico, history begins with the vague outline of an ancestor named Philippe Mius d'Entremont. Descendants evoke his memory like a spirit at a seance, like the beginning of a miracle. It is their own name that weaves through three centuries of sorrow and triumph.

Philippe d'Entremont was born in 1609. He had grown up on the exotic legends of Indians and coureurs de bois, his boy's mind swelling with imaginings. L'acadie was over a hundred years old when he arrived—named by Italian explorer Giovanni de Verrazanno, looking for a passage to China for the French king in 1524, claimed by Jacques Cartier. Samuel de Champlain and François Gravé Du Pont had nosed in for furs; then Pierre Du Gua de Monts had led the first sixty-nine settlers to St. Croix in 1604, where half of them died of scurvy. Philippe had been a child learning his catechism in Normandy when L'acadie's first log homes were hoisted up. At forty-three, he set his own tall boots on L'acadie.

It was a fierce land and green, startling his senses awake. Minds accustomed to the sure lines of cobbled roads and the symmetry of civilized France stuttered at the hugeness. Here the land dwarfed an empire's century of effort. Perhaps Philippe could see the shape of greatness not yet built. Perhaps he sensed something darker swirling beneath the obvious. In 1651, the place was already complicated.

L'acadie was a half-century deep in intrigue and the leapfrogging ambitions of the French Royal court. Avarice had already deformed the fate of the place. D'Entremont might have glimpsed that on his crossing over. He'd come at the urging of Charles de la Tour, the wily, renegade

French fur trader who'd been longing for his lost governorship. When his old rival died, de la Tour had ingratiated himself at court and returned to Acadia as governor. Resurrection was one of the benedictions of the New World.

D'Entremont was de la Tour's lieutenant, a cushy privilege that lifted his wife and their children a little above the backbreaking life of a colony. But Madame d'Entremont's eyes must have widened at the scruffy look of Port-Royal. It was a puny capital, all wood, beam and thatch, with none of the stone and masonry of France. The people here were no longer French, but Acadian—shaggy coureurs de bois with their furs and Mi'kmaq wives, and farmers in home-woven clothes with their bushels of grain to be milled. The women still covered their heads with Norman caps, their *capines,* and everyone wore wooden shoes or *souliers sauvage,* moccasins. The wives were younger here and had many more children than in France. They were fearless travelling in their canoes. It was a basic existence and every part of life was coaxed from the land: soap was made with fat and ash, tobacco pouches with animal bladders, mattresses with straw. Acadians often traded illegally with the English colonies for the things they couldn't make—firearms, fancy textiles and sophisticated tools and implements.

There were no grand churches yet, just wooden structures where superstition and Catholicism blended pious prayers with a belief in sorcerers and *la chasse galerie* —witchy night riders. Acadians knew that animals spoke on Christmas Eve and no one in the colony butchered or ploughed on All Souls' Day for fear of wounding the dead. But hands and minds were practical in the skills of survival and native wisdom. The Acadians had learned from the Indians, had been rescued by them in those first, foodless winters. The Mi'kmaq taught them to stuff *machekoui,* birch bark, into their walls for insulation, to brew spruce beer to ward off scurvy and to collect plantain to use as a salve. The Acadians learned to hunt with dogs like the natives. This was the astonishing bare-bones life that stared back at the d'Entremonts.

For two years Philippe stayed in Port-Royal as the governor's man: legal counsellor, keeper of the garrison, counter of goods—the *lieutenant général* and *procureur général.* There were papers to sign and notes to be sealed in the name of the Crown, and always an ear to the sound of approaching armies. He had long days with quill in hand and long discussions about the shape of the colony's economy. L'acadie was changing. The original fur and export trade of the old coureurs de bois was moving west, to the new centre of Montreal. A more local economy was taking hold, families of blacksmiths, millers and coopers serving families of farmers and fishermen, keeping their money home. Becoming a nation.

In 1653, de la Tour rewarded d'Entremont with the seigneury of Pobomcoup, or Pubnico, at Cape Sable. It was a wild swatch of land, not yet farmed—more curse than blessing. Over twenty years Philippe carved out a farming and fishing village along its harbour and fathered a dynasty that would wind around nearly all the Acadian élite. He learned to live and thrive in the menacing thicket of unsettled land, winning over the resentments of lower-down, working people. Baron d'Entremont's feudal domain was rare in L'acadie. People here, away from the fussy court of French entitlement, had grown wild as wind.

Acadians had little use for grand titles or even government. The constant act of survival made man's law seem brutal and punitive, and upper-class privileges undeserved. Acadians refused to be bullied by bureaucrats and tax collectors who ruled the peasant French in other places. Besides, the few seigneurs who did exist were lax about their traditional duties. They rarely built mills and bake-ovens or meted out justice, but acted like landlords, demanding their *cens et rentes*—rents. None of them ever demanded *corvée*—the customary tariff on fishing, timber cutting or use of common grazing pastures, perhaps knowing what the response would be.

Acadians relied on their own informal cooperativeness, electing panels to settle arguments over farm boundaries and stray cows, sometimes enlisting parish priests to serve as arbiters. But nothing could assuage the tyranny of geography.

L'acadie was sandwiched between the British and Dutch colonies to the south and French ones to the northwest. It stood or crumpled according to the wars of other nations, a fact every generation of d'Entremont had to live with. It had already been lost once to the English who'd brought in Scottish settlers and renamed it Nova Scotia. Ten years later they'd returned it as payment for King Charles's dowry debt to France. Now the tide was bringing the English in again.

Oliver Cromwell, Lord Protector of England, ordered his Colonial troops in Massachusetts to clear out the French. It was a sweeping edict that sent his Boston fleet swooping into Port-Royal in 1654. The news travelled through Acadia, panicking d'Entremont. But Pubnico was too far away and the enemy never arrived. De la Tour wasn't so lucky—the British dragged him back to England as a prisoner.

De la Tour, the consummate wheeler-dealer, eventually pried his release from Cromwell and skulked back to Cape Sable, where he eventually died. But L'acadie was being jostled between two rival nations, like a mouse in a cat's paws. For the next thirteen years France and England appointed their own governors to preside simultaneously —confounding locals with contradictory policies. No wonder Acadians disliked government.

Acadians began abandoning Port-Royal for the north and southeast, searching for land and safety. The French court at Versailles couldn't protect them from Britain and its American colonies. L'acadie returned to French possession under the Treaty of Breda, but peace was brief.

D'Entremont's seigneury of Pobomcoup was steadily growing. Twenty-five families had clustered onto Philippe's settlement by the early 1670s, including two of de la Tour's sons, who had married the daughters of their father's old lieutenant. The second generation of d'Entremonts was growing up Acadian. Philippe's oldest daughter, Marguerite, married into the Melanson family, and prospered in Port-Royal. Then in 1675, the Dutch attacked the coastline.

Dutch troops made surprise raids along the southern shore of L'acadie. They ransacked French posts along the

Bay of Fundy. When they moved inland, the d'Entremonts were vulnerable. The Dutch fired on Philippe, chasing his livestock and burning his barns with their torches. Then they moved north, taking Governor Jacques de Chambly prisoner, and claiming Acadia for Holland. Who the hell would crawl out of the woods or the sea next?

D'Entremont was in his mid-sixties by then, not able to fight or run on old legs. After twenty years of effort, he'd been forced out of his own village of Pubnico. It was the first taste of exile, the bitter tearing away that would haunt so many d'Entremonts and so many Acadians. Philippe put his sons in charge of his baronetcy and moved in with his daughter and her husband, Pierre Melanson, in Port-Royal. He probably knew he'd never return. He left behind his name, his land and his sons—a final curse against the Dutch and the English.

Eventually Philippe's daughter and son-in-law founded Grand Pré, and the old man followed them there. The colony would become an Acadian stronghold and the debarkation point for thousands of Acadians during *le grand dérangement*—the Deportation. It was the final horror Philippe would not live to see.

Philippe's last good years were lived in the comfort of his daughter's family. Her husband, Pierre, had thirty-one head of cattle and an arsenal of twelve guns—a small fortune in the colony. A few years later Pierre would be named major in charge of the militia when war erupted between England and France. Again, the Acadians were wedged between two nations.

In 1690, 400 British troops came ashore at Port-Royal, disarming the tiny garrison. Acadians were shoved into the church and forced to swear oaths of allegiance to the King of England, then thirty homes were set on fire. L'acadie became part of Massachusetts by royal proclamation. France sent in its own commandant, coercing oaths of allegiance to the French Crown in exchange for food and wine. At least the Acadians made a meal of it. But it would be seven more years before the colony belonged to France again under the Treaty of Ryswick. The truth was, it belonged only to itself.

At the beginning of a new century, d'Entremont's children's children were raising families. Some had married into the Mi'kmaq nation and their children were Métis. The family seigneury at Pubnico was fattening on good yields of peas and wheat and on lots of cattle. There was a water mill, too. Philippe was ninety-one when he died in Grand Pré. There was no undertaker; a male relative washed his body and dressed it in fine clothing. He was laid out in his daughter's house for two nights, and by the light of a single candle he was waked in the low murmur of prayers and hymns. Then Philippe was carried in his coffin to church, accompanied by priests who sang the songs of the dead. For many years after, his family tended his grave, pulling up weeds and adorning it with small white pebbles plucked from the shore. It was the Mi'kmaq way, learned by the Acadians.

But only the dreams of the dead are peaceful. The living were left to the British and their colonials, plundering L'acadie and bleeding it with economic blockades. France finally gave up all its forts and territories in Hudson Bay, Newfoundland and Acadia to the British under the Treaty of Utrecht of 1713. Acadians had no choice but to surrender and darkness fell. Religious orders from France were no longer permitted in the colony—only priests from Quebec could educate and administer the rites of the church. Fewer and fewer children received schooling. Illiteracy increased and L'acadie receded into the blankness of occupation. Britain demanded loyalty, but still the d'Entremonts and other Acadians refused the unequivocal oath of allegiance, preferring neutrality. The lessons of history had been explicit: no one could predict which nation would dominate; only that Acadians would be squeezed in the middle. They signed an open allegiance to England, promising not to bear arms for or against the Crown.

Through forty years of occupation the Acadians lived quietly under the shadow of British law. The d'Entremonts spread across L'acadie, expanding their settlement in Pubnico and rooting firmly among the other families of Grand Pré. They lived and died in the sureness of their faith and superstitions, in their old world modesties, refusing modern dress and the Quebec custom of public kissing. They lived among themselves, separate from the occupiers. In 1754, they became the enemy again.

The Seven Years War erupted in Great Meadows, Pennsylvania, the decisive battle between French and English for possession of North America. Old suspicions were aroused. The British ambushed the French fort of Beauséjour at the head of the Bay of Fundy in June of

1755. Unfortunately, 300 Acadian conscripts were discovered inside the walls. Clearly, they couldn't be trusted in a war between the rivals. Charles Lawrence, the English lieutenant-governor of Nova Scotia, became belligerent.

Lawrence summoned Acadian deputies to Halifax and demanded they take the oath. They clung to the condition of their arms exemption. Lawrence jailed them and began setting a trap for the expulsion of thousands of Acadians. Deportation was Lawrence's idea, in violation of his own government and the long-standing articles of French capitulation, which had recognized Acadian neutrality. But 300 Acadians had been caught taking sides.

The roundup began at Fort Beauséjour and spread across the three maritime provinces. In Philippe's last home of Grand Pré, four companies of American Colonials arrived with orders to lure the Acadians onto waiting ships, deport them, then burn their property to the ground. They posted a summons in the churchyard ordering men and boys to attend the reading of the King's orders. Four hundred unsuspecting Acadians gathered, some d'Entremont descendants among them, as the soldiers closed in. The American commander delivered the horrible news:

> Your Lands and Tennements, Cattle...and Live Stock of all Sortes are Forfitted to the Crown with all your other Effects....That it is Preremtorily his Majesty's orders That the whole French Inhabitants of these Districts, be removed...and hope that in what Ever part of the world you may Fall you may be Faithful

> Subjects, a Peasable and happy People. I Must also inform you That it is his Majesty's Pleasure that you remain in Security under the Inspection and Direction of the Troops that I have the Honr. To Command.

It was a mass deportation, suddenly and efficiently executed. Acadian men were routed at bayonet point, bait for the women and children who would surely follow. They were herded along the shore, the sound of their grief snatched away by the wind. Adults prayed, children cried and the sky filled with whispered farewells and the screams of mothers. Women were yanked from their children's arms, husbands ripped from their wives. There was no time to think or to plan; minds froze on the sudden terror and surprise, on the last stolen look at home. *"C'est ne pas vrai, c'est ne pas possible. C'est une erreur."* It wasn't true, it wasn't possible, it had to be a mistake.

Erreur, errer, c'est le même chose—to err or to wander meant the same thing in their language. All they had built, all they had worked for, was suddenly forfeit. Acadia did not exist; they did not exist. And so they would wander.

Acadians swore to remember that day forever; to hand it down to their children's children's children. They would never, ever forget the place called home. Then they vanished onto the sea.

About 6,000 Acadians were deported in the fall of 1755. The expulsion continued over the next eight years as small groups of Acadians were captured or gave themselves up to follow the search for families lost in exile. In the end, almost three-quarters of the Acadian population of 15,000 disappeared, their land and buildings scorched. Philippe d'Entremont's great-grandchildren were forced out of Grand Pré and deported. His seigneury of Pubnico was raided twice; in 1756, seventy-two men, women and children were herded and sent to Boston. And in 1759 a group of stragglers were taken prisoner and shipped off to France, never to be heard from again. The d'Entremont name was completely erased from the place.

Dividing and scattering Acadians among Britain's thirteen colonies was supposed to force them into assimilation, to dilute whatever stain they were accused of having. The British didn't count on memory or on the fierce determination that marginalization taught.

Everywhere they went in the Colonies, the Acadians were hated—Catholics in a Puritan country, French traitors among English loyalists. They were refused work, land, medicine; even burial. Often they starved. Sometimes villages weren't even notified that Acadians would be arriving; townspeople were aghast to find hundreds of them huddling on their wharves. The Acadians hobbled through the colonies, weary and unwanted. Like the d'Entremonts, some landed in Massachusetts; others eventually arrived in Louisiana. Many stayed clustered in the French colony of the South, elbowing a place among the French Créoles who'd been there since the seventeenth century. The Créoles, meaning local or not imported, to distinguish themselves from other French blow-ins, looked down their noses at the Acadian peasants. The Acadians thought they were *mon fils-de-putain riche*—son-of-a-bitch aristocrats. Over the years they hung onto their language and ways, becoming a people called Cajuns. It was the sound of Anglo-Americans trying to pronounce *L'acadiens*.

Some Acadians resisted deportation and fled into the woods with their families, or to Quebec. Others clung to the hope of returning to the land that had spit them out, and almost immediately began the long journey back to L'acadie. For years the d'Entremonts and their people wandered the world like a lost tribe, through England, France and the United States. And then suddenly, they were no longer a threat.

Acadians were officially given permission to resettle in Nova Scotia in 1764. The war was over and France had given up her empire in North America. Everything had been won and lost on Quebec's Plains of Abraham in 1759. The fate of Canada had been decided. France had ceded Quebec and Acadia.

The d'Entremonts began their cautious return in 1767, settling in Pubnico. But the seigneury was gone; the farms Philippe and his family had cleared were occupied by other, English settlers. Philippe's descendants had to build on uncleared land in Pubnico-West and East. They had to begin again, along with other Acadian families—the Amiraults, Belliveaus, Duons and Mius. Perhaps the d'Entremonts were more stubborn than the others, or more lucky. They were one of the few Acadian families to return to the very lands they'd been expelled from. It is on their bones that Pubnico survives today.

The road to full citizenship took over a century. Nova Scotian laws prevented Catholics like the d'Entremonts from establishing schools or voting. Formal education didn't begin until the early 1800s. There was no educated elite and no mother country to supply Acadians with teachers and priests. They relied on Quebec missionaries until their first resident priest arrived in 1799. West Pubnico didn't have its own church until 1815. Literacy stalled and even prominent men like justice of the peace, Benoni d'Entremont, could barely write his name, let alone official papers.

The ironies of history cut like bayonets. Returning exiles competed for land with the flood of newly arrived United Empire Loyalists. Those who had given them so little comfort in their exile were now fleeing the American Revolution and taking the best sections of land. Nothing was ever certain for Acadians.

Inch by inch, the d'Entremonts burrowed back into the land they had lost, and Acadians slowly won the rights of belonging. It was a d'Entremont from Pubnico who was the first Acadian elected in the Maritimes. Simon d'Entremont took his seat in the house in 1837, along with Frédéric Robichaud.

Ten years later, a forgotten people were remembered by the American poet, Henry Wadsworth Longfellow. In his epic poem of Acadia, "Evangeline," he stoked the embers of ethnic pride and focused the world's attention on the deportation and its haunting hurts.

Many a weary year had passed since the burning of Grand-Pre,
When on the falling tide the freighted vessels departed,

Bearing a nation, with all its household goods, into exile,
Exile without an end, and without an example in story.
Far asunder, on separate coasts, the Acadians landed;
Scattered were they, like flakes of snow when the wind from the northeast
Strikes aslant through the fogs that darken the Banks of Newfoundland.
Friendless, homeless, hopeless, they wandered from city to city

Acadians had a symbol and rallied around it. They erected a statue of the fictional heroine, Evangeline, in Grand Pré, the village where Philippe had died.

Twelve generations after Philippe Mius d'Entremont planted his family in L'acadie, Pubnico flourishes and waves its Acadian flag. It is a chin thrust to the fates more than a fist. Philippe's people are still here, still speaking French, still stiffening through the deprivations of Lent. Many of them work the fisheries now. They huddle together in the long winters to argue the facts of their survival, impaling each other on the quick wit of their French ancestors who started the Order of Good Cheer four centuries before. They beat back the cold with their own good humour and optimism.

The people of Pubnico scour the region for clues, beach-combing its edges with their metal detectors and compasses, plotting their past like a delicious mystery, like tourists in another time. Comparing their discoveries. Somewhere in this land might be the buried stones of d'Entremont's grist mill or manor house—the hard, cold proof that Acadians existed before deportation, that they were makers of history not simply its victims. These are the shards that the local sleuths hanker for—amateur historians and anthropologists who speak of the long dead with the familiarity of family. And with the grins of irreverent pride. They are the descendants of Philippe Mius d'Entremont, and they know, as the land does, that they are planted deeper down than the boots of Britain could ever stamp out.

It is a memory that does not hate and does not forgive. It is simply a denial of amnesia and dilution. It is the hoisting up of children onto the shoulders of existence, Acadian children—as far as the eye can see. And as far back as the beginnings of this country.

Acadian Immigration History in Canada

Philippe Mius d'Entremont arrived in Nova Scotia in 1651, more than a century after Jacques Cartier had nosed into the New World. In 1534, Cartier had left St. Malo with two ships looking for a route to China. He eventually wintered near the Iroquois village of Stadacona in Quebec, taking possession of Canada in the name of French King Francis I.

The first French colonists in Acadia arrived in 1604 under the leadership of Governor Pierre Du Gua de Monts. A distinguished member of the French Court of Henry IV, he'd been granted a fur-trade monopoly through the de Monts Trading company, the first chartered company in Canada. De Monts's instructions were to populate, cultivate and fortify the area, convert the Indians and carry on trade with them for a ten-year period. He arrived with his friends and partners, Samuel de Champlain and François Gravé Du Pont. They sailed around Cape Sable, entered the Bay of Fundy and named a small inlet Port-Royal. Then they crossed the bay, following a river to the island of St. Croix.

Here they hoisted up twelve buildings around an open court. The brutal North American winter crushed their efforts and colonial bickering over boundaries would soon lead to fatal clashes. Rivalries between the empires of France and Britain would ultimately result in an Acadian migration of another sort: the imposed expulsion of 1755. Both imperialistic arguments and harsh living conditions would play crucial roles in determining the culture and history of Acadia. No matter how complicated, emigration to the New World continued.

Almost thirty years after de Monts's efforts, the next wave of French immigrants arrived in 1632. Commander de Razilly set out from France with 300 men, his mind firmly set on developing the Acadian colony. Between 1632 and 1636, smaller numbers of settlers, both men and women, trickled into Acadia to lend a hand to the first colonists. By the eighteenth century the Acadian population along the St. Lawrence and the Atlantic coast numbered close to 15,000.

Overcoming Obstacles

Sieur de Monts's first settlement of Acadia in 1604 had about eighty colonists. But they were hopelessly ill-prepared. Food supplies dwindled, drinking water froze and firewood ran out. To add to their problems, settlers died of scurvy. The next year, the settlers moved to the shores of Port-Royal. They set up a fur-trading centre and began exchanging goods with the Indians. There were three Native tribes in the general area: about 5,000 Malecites in western New Brunswick, 10,000 Abenakis on the coast of what is now Maine and about 4,000 Mi'kmaq straddling Nova Scotia, P.E.I. and eastern New Brunswick. The Mi'kmaq became their staunchest friends and rescuers, supplying them with meat and the means to survive. Settlers began to cultivate the land and built a grist mill. This time the Acadians prepared for the cold, storing enough necessities to last them through the winter.

Here the French formed the first social club in North America, to help pass the long winter nights. They called it *l'Ordre de Bon Temps*, or the Company of Good Cheer.

Everyone took turns providing culinary delights and entertainment. Marc Lescarbot, a lawyer from Paris, staged the New World's first play in Port-Royal, *Le Théâtre de Neptune*. The performers were French settlers and natives; some played their roles from canoes in the harbour. Port-Royal flourished as a trading post but the venture was by no means secure.

In 1607, de Monts's monopoly on the fur trade was challenged and then cancelled. Members of the expedition went back to France. A few returned in 1610 but were raided in 1613 by the recently established English colonists of Jamestown, Virginia. This was the end of the French trading post and the beginning of the struggle between France and England for control of the area—an argument that would last more than a century.

France and Britain had been rivals for years. When both empires fixed their ambitions on colonizing North America, the existing tensions only increased. For the next hundred years the two countries were often at war, and their colonies had no choice but to follow along with them. On the French side, no colony would be more drastically affected than Acadia.

Acadia was strategically positioned between New England to the south and New France to the north, which made life perilous for the settlers. The English saw Acadia as a barrier to their final conquest of all North America. In 1621 the English government claimed Acadia as its own and changed its name to Nova Scotia, "New Scotland." In 1629 a Scottish settlement was set up on the shores of Port-Royal and a fort was built on the ruins of the French habitation. Settlers loyal to the British Crown began to farm the land. But in 1632 Britain's King Charles I recognized French ownership of Acadia, and ordered the Scottish settlers home. The territory continued to change hands until the Treaty of Utrecht in 1713, which permanently ceded Acadia to England.

The strife for the Acadians, however, was far from over. With their history of divided loyalties, they now found themselves subjects of Britain. Wanting to remain a distinct entity unto themselves they refused to take the oath of allegiance to the British Crown and offered instead an oath of neutrality. They also promised never to take up arms against either the British or the French, who were still continually clashing as colonists.

The British colonists went along with the Acadian's oath of neutrality until 1755 when the Halifax government gave the Acadians an ultimatum: either they declare their allegiance to Britain or they would face deportation from the colony. The Acadians remained true to their conviction of neutrality, and the British to their threat of expulsion. An estimated 10,000 Acadians were torn from their land, stripped of their belongings, separated from family and friends and deported. Their homes were burned to the ground and they were erased, as though they'd never existed. Some were shipped to France and England. Many ended up in Louisiana and never came back. Others fled to Quebec, or into the woods for their lives.

The political motivation of the Great Expulsion was obvious. By scattering the Acadians among Britain's

Thirteen Colonies along the Atlantic, the Acadians would be immersed in English society and culture and forced to assimilate. They would no longer be a threat to Britain's colonial empire. But the Acadians had learned from history to be a tenacious people. Holding strong to the values of self-reliance and determination they fought to rekindle and preserve the Acadian legacy.

The Acadian Legacy

After the Great Expulsion, and even after being allowed to return to their homeland of Acadia in 1763, the Acadians struggled for basic civil liberties. Clearly, their most immediate objective was survival; their lifestyle was one of subsistence. Little by little they re-established themselves, and by Confederation in 1867, they numbered some 87,000. At the turn of the century the Acadian population was at 140,000 and by 1981, 251,000 New Brunswick Acadians represented thirty-six percent of the province's population and 15,000 made up almost thirteen percent of P.E.I.'s population.

As their numbers grew, so too did the strength and confidence of their distinctive culture and heritage. Acadian pride had never faltered and in the mid-1800s it was further invigorated by a now-famous poem. In 1847 American poet Henry Wadsworth Longfellow published "Evangeline." He had heard the story of the expulsion and was able to capture its power and feeling in verse. For the Acadians, the poem—although a fictional interpretation of the Acadian experience—had a tremendous impact and bolstered their sense of self-worth. Long a neglected people, they were now the focus of widespread and sympathetic attention. With the Acadian folk heroine of Evangeline to mark their past, the Acadians moved on toward building a future.

Perhaps the next major step forward for the Acadian community came in July of 1867 with the publication of the first French-language newspaper in the Maritimes. *Le Moniteur Acadian* gave Acadians a way of communicating and generating ideas. Another fortification of their identity came in the 1880s when an Acadian association was formed. An Acadian flag was designed and a national day of festivity inaugurated.

Philippe Mius d'Entremont could never have imagined what lay ahead for his people and the enormous price of freedom and distinctiveness. Through the centuries of sorrow and victory, d'Entremont's village of Pubnico still stands. Several generations of his ancestors join in the annual festivities to celebrate the struggle the Acadians have endured. Above all else, the d'Entremont clan and all Acadians celebrate perseverance. It is a refusal to become part of the melting pot, to be meshed into a commonality, and a fierce preference to remain distinctly Acadian.

Sources

Acadia of the Maritimes: Thematic Studies from the Beginning to the Present, Jean Daigle, editor. Chaire d'études L'acadiennes, Université de Moncton, New Brunswick, 1995.

Acadia: The Geography of Early Nova Scotia to 1760, Andrew Hill Clark. University of Wisconsin Press, Madison, 1968.

The Acadian Exiles: A Chronicle of the Land of Evangeline, Arthur Doughty. Brook, Toronto, 1916.

Acadian Spirit, directed by Peter d'Entremont and Lindalee Tracey. White Pine Pictures, Toronto, 1998.

Acadians, Barry Moody. Grolier, Toronto, 1981.

The Acadians: Creation of a People, Naomi Griffiths. McGraw-Hill Ryerson, Toronto, 1973.

The Acadians of Nova Scotia: Past and Present, Sally Ross and J. Alphonse Deveau. Nimbus, Halifax, 1992.

The Atlantic Provinces: The Emergence of Colonial Society, 1712–1857, W. Stewart MacNutt. McClelland & Stewart, Toronto, 1965.

Cajun Country, Barry Jean Ancelet, Jay Edwards and Glen Pitre. University Press of Mississippi, Mississippi, 1991.

The Canadian Encyclopedia, World Edition. McClelland & Stewart, Toronto, 1998.

The Country of Acadia, Melvin Gallant; Elliot Shek, translator. Simon and Pierre, Toronto, 1986.

The Fitzhenry & Whiteside Book of Canadian Facts & Dates, Jay Myers. Fitzhenry & Whiteside, Richmond Hill, 1991.

History of the Acadians, Bona Arsenault. Leméac, Montreal, 1978.

A Land of Discord Always: Acadia from Its Beginning to the Expulsion of Its People, 1604–1755, Charles D. Mahaffie Jr. Down East Books, Maine, 1995.

A Proper Acadian, Mary Alice Downie and George Rawlyk. Kids Can Press, Toronto, 1980.

Father Bernard McGauran

Chapter Two

The Force of Hope: Father Bernard McGauran

Canada and the World in 1847

John A. Macdonald enters the cabinet for the first time as receiver-general.

Lord Elgin announces that Britain will give control of the post office to the provincial legislature.

John Franklin, of the Franklin Expedition, which searched for the Northwest Passage through the Arctic, dies aboard his ship in Victoria Strait.

Telegraph service is established between Montreal and Toronto.

The first zoo in Canada is established in Halifax.

Gold is discovered in California.

The Mormons found Salt Lake City.

Alexander Graham Bell, inventor of the telephone, is born in Scotland.

American poet Henry Wadsworth Longfellow publishes "Evangeline," a narrative poem about the Acadian expulsion.

Charlotte Brontë publishes *Jane Eyre;* Emily Brontë publishes *Wuthering Heights.*

Kitchen matches, revolvers, sewing machines and pekoe tea are available.

In 1847, the wet wool smell of winter clung to Quebec City long past Palm Sunday and Holy Week. Spring thaw was late—the St. Lawrence River wouldn't crack open until

May. Barricaded behind winter, the city knelt stiffly through Easter penitence, black silhouette against white snow.

Few distractions infiltrated the Catholic season of abstinence—the whiff of hot cross buns wafting from the convents, the muffled chatter of neighbours in the pews. But darker whisperings crept through the parishes that winter, worries about the sick and hungry Irish who had crossed the sea last year and rumours of a worsening Irish famine. Only winter offered protection against the emigrants—ice alone held them back. But the St. Lawrence would eventually have to thaw.

The Irish news reached beyond the old city walls to a small parish in Saint-Francois-de-Lac. Bernard McGauran was the new curate, *Father* McGauran now—a soft, wet-eyed priest. He stood at the altar clutching a pastoral letter from Archbishop Signay. Like parish priests all over Quebec, he'd been instructed to plead for pennies and prayers for Ireland. It made his heart lean homeward.

Bernard had come to Quebec in the 1830s before the Act of Union had renamed Lower Canada, Canada East. He had come on soft feet, leaving only a vague trail along his path to the grey stone seminary in Sainte-Anne-de-la-Pocatiére and to his ordination. He was born in Sligo, Ireland, in 1821—a county fattened by the linen and textile trade. Sligo was one of the great northern emigration ports sending well-fed emigrants to fill the colonies. Merchants like Bernard's father could afford the fifty shillings passage over. Now the south was spitting out hungrier emigrants and raggedy crowds were hurrying into steerage.

> *Le Canadien,* April 16, 1847: The news from Ireland is still sad. Cork is the county where famine and sickness reign the most cruelly....Emigration from the British Isles, and from Ireland in particular towards this continent is readying on a vast scale.

The Famine Irish had begun arriving the summer before. Thirty-two thousand of them had stumbled through the province, most of them poor and hollowed out. Many headed south to Montreal, Toronto and the United States. Some remained in Quebec over winter, obvious as sores in their shabby cloaks and shawls. With the famine spreading, parishes like McGauran's were reading terrible news about food riots and overcrowded poor houses; about corpses lying coffinless in the streets of Ireland.

On April 23, a "Citizen" wrote to *Le Canadien:* "In a few short weeks Ireland will be jettisoning onto our shores their hungry and dying hordes. If these immigrants bring with them germs of contagious diseases, I ask you, what will be the fate of Quebec and Montreal?"

The government deliberated over public safety. If emigration was going to be anything like last year, the Irish had to be stopped at the quarantine station at Grosse Ile, downriver from Quebec. They had to be lined up and examined, the sick separated from the well, perhaps even the dead from the living. Whatever contagions they carried would have to be contained. With improvements to the lower St. Lawrence almost complete, the whole country lay vulnerable to waterway traffic and disease.

The medical superintendent for Grosse Ile warned Governor General Elgin to expect more sick than the year before. Dr. Douglas requested extra funds to expand the station's facilities and to recruit more doctors. He was a veteran of the previous year's influx, and knew its patterns. Emigration usually swelled in July and August. If the numbers really bulged, he'd have time to build up his facility.

Public opinion wasn't so optimistic, dividing along the fault lines of fear. People had seen the ravages of smallpox and cholera and knew to be afraid. In the public imagination, the Irish became horrifying, their human shape obscured by their disease and poverty. Compassion competed with survival, superstition with faith. Father McGauran had only pity for the emigrants. "Victims of the greed of their landlords," he wrote to Archbishop Signay, "who send them on a painful journey, with food amounting to hardly a pound of either potatoes, or flour, or corn."

Cautious hearts finally did creak open. The thought of fellow Catholics on their knees, eating grass to stay alive, blunted the sharper edges of national interest.

> *Le Canadien,* April 28, 1847: God forbid that we should wish to close the doors of Canada to the unfortunate immigrants of Ireland. We hope that Canadians will be more generous, more hospitable, and more Christian than their neighbours to the south. The United States have adopted strict and isolationist measures which shift the tide of immigration away

from the American union, but which is now thrown upon the shores of Canada.

When the St. Lawrence finally opened, Dr. Douglas hurried to the quarantine station on Grosse Ile. Additional doctors, nurses, boatmen and police officers began preparations. Buildings were whitewashed and boats patched and readied. A few days later the chief emigration agent warned Lord Elgin that thirty-four ships were en route to Quebec, over 10,000 Irish passengers huddled in their holds.

The church mobilized, making plans for the Catholic missionary on Grosse Ile, and looking for a priest to lead it. Archbishop Signay decided on twenty-six-year-old, Irish-born Bernard McGauran. It was a good choice, and an honour. It was also a sentence more than a mission.

The quarantine station was thirty miles downstream from Quebec, a half-day's journey by steamer. Grosse Ile wasn't big. Barely a mile and a half long, it jutted out of the river like a stone thumb, ancient and insolent. Closer up its body softened under fir trees and birch.

On shore there was well-scrubbed order and efficiency. Sheds and hospitals stood neatly in rows, while more were under construction. Two hundred beds were ready for the sick, 100 more than the previous year. And there was enough room in the sheds for 800 healthy passengers.

Father McGauran found his chapel behind the hospitals. His own room was in a wooden house at the back. He bent into his prayers, thanking God for His love, confessing his own, asking for strength. And the blessings of Mary.

On Friday, May 14, the first ship of the season put anchor, her deck crowded with weary, squinting faces. The *Syria* had taken forty-six days to lurch across from Liverpool. Nine of her passengers had already died, fifty-two had dysentery and ship fever. Sailors hurried to pull the sick out of the hold and row them to shore. The healthy ones were lodged in the sheds.

Father McGauran's first religious act was a tender one. Little Owen Woods, born at sea, was baptized in the chapel. But there was no time to linger; the hospitals were filling up fast. Within days, over 200 of the *Syria's* passengers were lying in beds, perhaps Owen's own parents among them. Within a week, almost 4,000 more emigrants arrived, 800 of them sick. They were feverish and skeletal, and very quiet. There were no more beds for the sick, or sheds for the healthy.

Grosse Ile descended into chaos. The dead and dying spilled out of buildings, lying on rocks or on the beach where sailors left them. Sheds were converted into hospitals and healthy passengers were pushed out into the open, or kept aboard ships. Every day more boats delivered their wounded. The St. Lawrence choked on a flotilla of death ships, the vessels stretching two miles down river. But no one had counted on typhus; no one knew that it was spread by lice. Throughout the summer, two in ten passengers would die on their way to Canada. Some argued that they were the lucky ones.

Father McGauran hurried between sick beds, stumbling up and down the rocky ledges of Grosse Ile. He didn't sleep. He started to think that the station might need a priest for every ship. Already the arithmetic was boggling. He wrote to Archbishop Signay:

> I hasten to give you a few notes on the very sad state of Grosse Ile. Tonight we can count seven hundred sick in the hospitals, all in desperate condition. Doctor Douglas does not want to receive any more on the islands; since we truly have no place for them, he forces the captains to keep them on board, and we have at present thirty-two of these vessels which are like floating hospitals, where death makes the most frightful inroads, and the sick are crowded in among the more healthy, with the result that all are victims to this terrible sickness.

Father McGauran began to chafe under the authority of the island's doctor, and at the bumbling slowness of bureaucracy. His mission was clear, at least to himself. He'd been sent to Grosse Ile to save souls and lives, if he could. But people were dying unnecessarily, healthy passengers forced to wait on infected ships. McGauran pleaded with the authorities to land the well passengers, maybe on the farm land at the east end of the island. Nothing happened quickly enough.

There was difficulty getting aboard the ships and McGauran harangued the authorities for a skiff to get to the boats anchored off Grosse Ile. The dying needed him. McGauran was well liked, respected both on the island and by the ships' captains. They sensed the kindness behind his fury and forgave his occasional crankiness.

Day and night McGauran administered the Latin comforts of the Church, offering the Sacrament of Extreme Unction for the sick on board: *"Pax huic domui. Et omnibus habitantibus in ea"*—Peace be unto this house. And unto all who dwell in it.

He moved from bed to bed, giving out communion wafers from his gold cylindrical pix. If the crowds were too big, he dangled his crucifix for the Irish to kiss. But the imminence of death often hurried McGauran; he abbreviated the rites for the dying, hearing last confession and absolving them by anointing their foreheads with Holy Water. And then finally, the Last Blessing. *"Benedicat te omnipotens Deus, Pater, et Filius, et Spiritus Sanctus. Amen"*—May God Almighty bless thee: the Father, and the Son, and the Holy Ghost.

It was heart-wrenching work and a test of faith. The dying lingered for his arrival, pulling themselves up onto trembling elbows. Some only blinked an eye or waved a limp hand. The church's Last Blessing was the single epiphany that kept them alive, the small mercy of a priest and of absolution. The final human sound they heard was the Exhortation—God's welcome at the hour of their death: "My dear friend.…God is not only your judge, but He is also a tender father, whose love for you is infinite....Look, therefore, upon this earth as a land of exile, and let your thoughts and your sighs be directed to heaven...where God shall wipe away all tears from your eyes; where there shall be no more sorrow, no more sickness, no more death."

In all their misery and deprivation, McGauran marvelled how the Irish kept hold of their good manners and gratitude. How quietly they ached. Their small dignities made them more pitiful. And more worth rescuing. He wrote of his contentment to the archbishop. "I assure you, My Lord, that I have never felt so much consolation in my entire life, the blessings bestowed on us by the sick and the dying soften our hardships."

But the filth of the ships frightened McGauran. Disease has a terrible stench, and a foreignness that disrupts the soul. As good as the best ships were, their holds were sticky with muck and excrement, sometimes inches deep. There was no privacy or modesty. Chamber pots overflowed, bodies reeked from weeks without bathing, whole families perched together on damp planks of wood. Always, someone was holding on to someone else—mothers curling around cold babies, husbands weeping at the frozen gaze of dead wives, the abandoned clinging to each other.

Father McGauran bent into the stink of his own people, into the terrible murmur of last wishes and lost hope. There was so little relief to offer, except death. McGauran held to his rituals tightly. There was only madness without them.

> Today I spent five hours in the hold of one of these where I administered the sacraments to a hundred people, while my very welcome colleague was on board another. It would be better to spend one's entire life in a hospital than to spend just a few hours in the hold of one of these vessels where there are so many people, and so many sick among them. It is there, My Lord,

> that we are in the most danger. While we are on the ships, there are people dying in the hospital without the sacraments. I have not taken off my surplice today; we meet people everywhere in need of the sacraments; they are dying on the rocks, and on the beach where they have been cast by the sailors, who simply could not carry them to the hospitals. We buried twenty-eight yesterday, twenty-eight today, and now (two hours past midnight), there are thirty dead whom we will bury tomorrow. I have not gone to bed for five nights. The spectacle, My Lord, is heart-rending. Once these hapless people are struck down by this strange malady, they lose all mental and physical powers and die in the most acute agony! We hardly give anyone Holy Communion, because we do not have time.

These Irish were the poorest of Ireland's poor—shoved out of the ports of Liverpool, Cork, Limerick, starved by the famine before they even boarded the boats. Now the ships became their coffins. It was the heartless side of commerce.

Ever since the Napoleonic Wars, timber ships had filled up in Quebec for Europe, but the Irish famine promised two-way profits. Ships hurried to fill up on passengers, including old tubs that should have been left to rot on the beaches. Their names were hopeful—Argo, Herald, Primrose, Progress—but light didn't reach below deck; or air. Crammed passengers lived like moles, on crumbs. There was not enough food and water, and the dead littered the ocean they travelled on. The Atlantic became the largest Irish graveyard.

The navigational season began to stretch infinitely in front of Father McGauran. Ten days after the first ship arrived, there were already 135 dead. In the whole cholera epidemic of 1834, only 115 people had perished. Hope faltered and hands worked without the mind's commands.

Whether through faith or the numbing of fatigue, McGauran wasn't afraid of the fever. He never felt happier than those first days, nor more useful. There was meaning to the work, a sense of purpose in easing the emigrants. Faith and the fleeting hand of a Roman Catholic priest was all they had to hold on to.

> Even though we know that we bring a measure of consolation and happiness to the immigrants, it is ironic that we can be unhappy that the prevailing east winds continue to drive so many vessels at the same time to our shores....Doctor Douglas fears that the numbers will increase for the present. My Lord, it is impossible that two priests will do, my legs are beginning to bother me, because I am always on my feet.

The church hurried relief to Grosse Ile, sending more priests to Father McGauran. Across Quebec, Catholic and Protestant clergy volunteered for eight-day missions. One after another they appeared on the island, Fathers Beaumont, Belanger, Cazeau, Harper, McGuirk, Moylan, O'Reilly, Taschereau, Reverends Mountain, Parkin, Sutton—forty-two Catholic priests in all, seventeen Protestant ones. Their horror blurred in the unrelenting demand of the sick and dying. Hearts paused for the children.

McGauran worried about the orphans; there were fifty by the end of May. He saw them wailing beside their dead parents, waiting, with the faith of childhood, for mothers to awake. Sometimes other women passengers, or the cooks, scooped them onto their hips. Often the orphans refused to be coaxed away, and got underfoot. Father Taschereau saw one child playing with its dead mother's hand.

McGauran knew that many would die, slipping into the listlessness of the fever. He had buried them already, babies without names, without kin to mourn and keen for them. It was the layman, Hilaire Giroux, who acted as a witness for the Catholic burials. But perhaps the Lord favoured the children most, surely He must. Suffer the little children to come unto Me.

But these were brooding thoughts that had to be checked. McGauran and his priests did what they could to lead the orphans to other mothers, slipping the women money to feed an extra mouth. There was never enough time, or kind words. Always they had to hurry to another task.

It was strange how the mind adjusted to the noise of death, reaching into it for instruction. Sound was a compass for Father McGauran—the banging oars of approaching rowboats, the small wails that lifted up and faltered, shovels scraping into the dirt. Only the sound of laughter disappeared. Even children knew not to laugh in the face of death. Sometimes sound failed completely under the roar of wind and storms. The mind strained to hear. Snapping back on itself, it became afraid. Only the incessantness of work pulled thoughts back.

On May 30, 1847, he reported to his archbishop:

> The *St. George* has just moored beside the ship where I have been hearing confessions for the last four hours. As for me, My Lord, I have gotten over my fatigue, not that I have been resting. But being used to it now, I do not feel as tired as I did in the beginning. Mortality increases on board the ships, we have buried almost fifty today taken from these vessels. But I still hope that matters will gradually improve. I beg you to excuse the state of this letter. I am writing it aboard a ship. I did not have enough time to go home because the steamboat is almost on its way. I remain your Grace's very devoted servant.

Death on board the waiting ships was at least twice as much as on shore. Passengers and crew fell to the fever, crumpling into heaps. The well ones recoiled, afraid to touch the corpses that piled up. Some crews refused to remove the dead—on the *Sisters out of Liverpool,* Captain Christian had to go down into the hold and carry the corpses on his back. The captain of the *Erin's Queen* bribed his sailors with a sovereign for each body they brought up.

Grosse Ile assumed the weary rhythms of a battlefield, organizing itself around the incoming casualties, and the worst cases of typhus. Hundreds of white canvas army tents began to dot the land, at first housing the healthy and then the sick. Rain and wind pummelled the tents, and the occupants floated in mud and sewage. One captain muttered hopelessly that it would be better to send a battery of artillery from Quebec, to sink the ships to the bottom rather than to let all the poor people die in such an agonizing manner. It was obvious that if things didn't change, they would all die.

The sick spread into every corner of available space, crammed two or three to a bed, along with the healthy. Even men and women lay together, modesty surrendered. Bunk beds were especially awful for the occupants of the lower beds, on which filth and muck rained down.

McGauran tried to keep the Catholic calendar, but the chapel had to be given over to the passengers of the *Agnes*. The priests erected a tent behind the sacristy for mass, but God's own word competed with the groaning of the sick. Finally, even that tent was snatched by the doctors. There was little room left for the soul's meagre comforts.

McGauran twisted on his own recriminations, fearful that he was letting down his office; that souls were dying unblessed. It was excruciating trying to organize his duties, to be in six places at the same time. Finally McGauran and the young Father Taschereau came to an agreement. Two priests would go to the hospitals, three to the ships, and the remaining man would attend to the burials and be available for urgent cases.

But McGauran was getting tired, run down, still refusing the pleas of the other priests to rest. By early June he was staggering from weakness and headaches. Father Taschereau mustered the courage to order him to bed and McGauran complied. But the next morning he stumbled aboard a few more ships. By afternoon he was feverish.

When Dr. Douglas was called, he warned the other priests not to speak of McGauran's illness, afraid, perhaps, of panic.

The dead kept stacking up. As McGauran faltered in his bed, wheelbarrows carted bodies past his window. Corpses were buried loosely, three in a hole, with barely a foot of earth to cover them. The smell was unbearable. Archbishop Signay gently advised the Irish to stay at home in a letter he sent to their bishops.

> The voice of religion and humanity imposes on me the sacred duty of exposing the dismal fate that awaits thousands of the unfortunate children of Ireland....During the passage, many of them have contracted fatal diseases and for the greater part, have thus become victims of an untimely death....I submit these facts to your consideration, that your Lordship may use every effort to dissuade your flock from immigrating in such numbers to Canada, and premature death.

Lice had burrowed into Father McGauran; *rickettsia prowazeki* lodged inside his blood vessels, incubating for those last ten days. On June 6 he was pulled aboard the steamer *St. George*. Thirsty and blurry headed, McGauran was transported to the General Hospital in Quebec City. He was kept clean and fed milk and light soups, but nobody had an exact cure—the disease itself wouldn't be understood for another fifty years. Father McGauran convulsed with the same delirium that had swallowed so many of the Irish emigrants. Typhus killed seventy percent of the time.

With seven of his priests sick with typhus, Archbishop Signay urged Lord Elgin to speed up construction of more hospitals—a fifth one had already filled up with emigrants. Helping hands were scarce—nurses and workmen refused to come to the island now, even for higher wages. And not enough was being done to separate the sick and healthy passengers.

Finally, tents were erected on the eastern part of the island, away from infection. It was what Father McGauran had demanded a month before. But bad luck followed as surely as rain. Emigrants had been spreading disease up river; the mayor of Montreal had died of typhus. The government had no choice but to impose longer quarantine, forcing healthy emigrants to stay for twenty days at Grosse Ile. Not surprisingly, typhus broke out in the eastern tents and priests were again administering last rites and burying 300 people a week.

The dying wouldn't stop on land or sea; funeral processions of small boats constantly unloaded their freight of corpses. On board ships, the grim business of separating the sick from the healthy ripped families apart.

One passenger, Robert Whyte, described the terrible scene:

> O God! May I never again witness such a scene as that which followed; the husband, the only support of an emaciated wife and helpless family—torn away forcibly from them, in a strange land; the mother

> dragged from her orphan children, that clung to her until she was lifted over the bulwarks, rending the air with their shrieks; children snatched from their bereaved parents, who were perhaps ever to remain ignorant of their recovery, or death. The screams pierced my brain; and the excessive agony so rent my heart, that I was obliged to retire to the cabin, where the mistress sat weeping bitterly.

By the end of August, the sticky heat was fading and night winds brought the first chill of autumn. Soon ice would scab over the place. Father McGauran returned to Grosse Ile with the bruised wisdom of a survivor. He knew the taste of typhus in his own mouth, and the terror of dying. It made him more tender. McGauran found the island calmer since summer; the tents had been taken down and he didn't have to tiptoe over bodies on the ground. McGauran moved less hurriedly through his chores. Though ships still waited to unload their holds, there were more hospitals and sheds for the emigrants now. The quarantine station slowly reasserted order, scrubbing away the squalor and hopelessness of the last few months. But in the wake of victory were the graves of mothers and fathers whose children remain unclaimed —their small, frightened eyes staring out into strangeness.

The priests brought the Irish children home to their parishes, sometimes twelve at a time. People crowded their churches, eager to adopt them—there were more families than orphans. They allowed the children to keep their last names—for some, it was all they had left. Over the generations their Irish names would stand out like orchids among the French ones, the small mercy of memory. Kellys, O'Brians, O'Connors, Murphys and Ryans weaving through French Quebec, many of their bearers unable to speak English, unable to point to where they'd come from in Ireland. But the names of their dead lived on. And if ghosts could be grateful, they would surely be to the Quebecers.

On September 16, Father McGauran again sent a note to Archbishop Signay:

> There is nothing new to report from the island, My Lord. Things follow their normal course. We have nine ships including three disembarking their passengers today and there are quite a few cases of smallpox. The number of deaths is approximately still the same....These last days, I fell victim to an attack of dysentery, but, with the help of God, I have recovered from it and I am perfectly well.

As fewer ships arrived, the hospitals and sheds emptied and emigrants moved more quickly through inspection. When they were finally cleared and their health bills signed, they were waved onto ships and down river to Montreal. It was the beginning of hope, and each boat sent up a cheer, and often a fiddler played. But crew and passengers turned sadly from the island of death, many of them leaving behind loved ones, or their dead. The sting of departure would mark each heart forever.

For the rest of the season, Father McGauran tended the ones left behind, offering blessings and last rites, listening to the private aches and pitiful regrets in their confessions. Perhaps the greatest grief was now, and grace, when one soul could contemplate another, unhurried by clamour and distraction. McGauran had time now to consider the whole person, to move the dying gently to the edge of the abyss, from where their milky eyes could see him last and go unafraid. These were his people, singular and human, not the squirming mass of disease, or the wailing souls of the summer before. Each one, God's gift and divinity. For many he bent the rules, cupping their grief like the hand of a friend. Gerald Keegan was one of the passengers Father McGauran helped, a man stumbling in grief, whose diary survived the summer.

> Eileen is dead....For three days I watched her as she went through spasms of wracking pain and fever.... This afternoon with bursting heart and throbbing head I knelt by as life ebbed out of her. I saw a priest....His name was Father McGauran, an Irishman. He came... said some prayers for the repose of my dear departed. He reminded me that hard as it may be, she would have to be buried without delay...the burial place was a field...where the dead were tossed five and six deep in trenches. I asked for a shovel, intending to dig a grave in a secret spot, mindful that the authorities wouldn't approve. Father McGauran got one...and helped me carry the body....There we reverently buried the most beautiful girl in all the world.

Twenty days later, Gerald Keegan died with Father McGauran beside him. He was buried beside his wife, Eileen.

So much was lost in the summer of sorrow, so many dreams ended there; so many dreamers buried. On November 1, Father McGauran celebrated All Saints' Day, commemorating the blessed in heaven. Perhaps he counted among them the thousands who had perished that summer. Maybe he believed that there was a special place set aside in heaven for the Irish of 1847.

That same day the last ship arrived at Grosse Ile. There was no heat on the island, nothing to keep the hospitals and sheds warm. Dr. Douglas wouldn't allow the passengers from the *Lord Ashburton* to land at the quarantine station. Father McGauran went on board, and then the passengers were put on steamers to Montreal. The dying was over. Two days later, the quarantine station closed for the season.

Almost 6,000 dead were officially counted that summer. Unofficially, it might have been as high as 20,000. No one could add up the bodies that fell in the woods or the river. Some days were too harrowing to count at all. Only the names of the buried were scratched into log books, beside their names—"cholera," "typhus," "cholera," "typhus."

By the end of the navigational season, 400 ships had sailed to Canada, carrying 100,000 emigrants. Of the forty-two Catholic priests who had worked there, nineteen contracted typhus and four died.

It took years for the Famine Irish to float up the St. Lawrence and root firmly in this country, years before their diseases and poverty were no longer feared. They went on to hoist up the bridges of Montreal and to help build the Lachine Canal. They moved to the Ottawa Valley, to Toronto and on westward, where their children grew up Canadian and helped build a nation, where Ned Hanlan became the world's champion rower, and Daniel John O'Donoghue and James Ryan helped forge the union movement. They became writers, farmers, bosses and workers, their Irish words braiding into Canadian English—wee, smidgen, finagle, shenanigans.

Father McGauran returned to Quebec City and helped build an orphanage and refuge for the Irish called St. Brigid's. He lived to see the two Canadas unite in Confederation, and the railways begin to move the Irish across the country. Thirty-five years after the summer of sorrow, Father Bernard McGauran died and was buried beneath a large Celtic cross in a cemetery in Sillery, near Quebec City.

On Grosse Ile, another Celtic cross stands sentry on a lonely, windswept ledge. Engraved on it are these words: "Sacred to the memory of the thousands of Irish emigrants who, to preserve the faith, suffered hunger and exile in 1847–48, and stricken with fever ended here their sorrowful pilgrimage."

Father McGauran was their friend and refuge in a time without hope. Perhaps it's what he'd come for, when he sailed across the sea from Ireland.

Irish Immigration History in Canada

Bernard McGauran left his home in County Sligo in the 1830s, to become a priest in Ste-Anne-de-la-Pocatiére, Quebec. A year after his ordination, the Irish potato famine sent thousands of desperate emigrants toward Quebec and into his care. But McGauran's arrival predates the Famine Irish and is part of the first and most significant wave of Irish immigrants to Canada: the period between 1825 and 1845.

However, while many people think of the Irish famine as the time "when the Irish came to Canada," an estimated 475,000 Irish landed in British North America before then. It was this earlier wave of Irish immigrants that would shape the development of Irish Canada and lay the most meaningful cultural foundations.

While many argue that the Irish explorer Brendan the Bold arrived before the Norse discovered Vinland, there's little but ethnic pride to support them. But the Irish have been arriving since the seventeenth century, mostly because of political and military links between France and southern Ireland. The Irish may have made up as much as five percent of the population of New France. Some French-Canadian and Acadian surnames are corrupted Irish ones: Riel (from Reilly) and Caissie (from Casey).

Early on the Irish had trickled into Newfoundland. Since the early eighteenth century, Bristol fishing ships had stopped at Wexford and Waterford to take on provisions and an Irish crew and labourers for the Newfoundland fishery. The Irish even had a name for Newfoundland in their own language—Talamh an Eisc—

a distinction they gave no other place in the New World. During the 1760s, they were joined by a group of Ulster Presbyterians who settled at Truro, Nova Scotia. An undetermined number of Irish were also part of the Loyalist migration.

There had been "emigration mania" two decades before the famine. The Irish economy had been declining while the population was exploding. Emigrants were mostly from Ireland's northern counties such as Ulster, north Connaught and north Leinster. They were middle class and could afford the voyage over to a second chance and a steadier future. It was an orderly emigration; most came in families, but there were also single male and female immigrants.

The majority of these newcomers bypassed Newfoundland and Halifax in favour of New Brunswick, Nova Scotia, P.E.I., Quebec and Ontario. The Irish spread throughout the countryside, partly because land from recent timber operations was cheap. Unlike the Scots or English, the Irish tended to huddle in ports like Halifax and Saint John, where they provided cheap labour. Even in rural districts, the Irish preferred to seek employment instead of, or in addition to, setting up farms. By the 1830s, Cumberland County in Nova Scotia, Kings, Queens, Carleton and Northumberland counties in New Brunswick; Queens in P.E.I.; and virtually the whole of Upper Canada east of Toronto and north of the older Loyalist settlements were distinctly Irish in character.

And then a terrible desperation changed the complexion of Irish immigration. The Great Irish Famine of

1846 to 1852 was a truly horrific human disaster and its resulting pall almost halved the population of 8,000,000 Irish. The potato crop fell to the blight and the Irish starved, waiting for a miracle. Poorhouses were overwhelmed, soup kitchens could not feed the hungry, hundreds of thousands died, orphans wandered motherless, and then cholera and typhus pulled the half-living into the fever pits—the mass graves. Emigration was the only hope. As many as 2,000,000 Irish fled their homeland and another 1,000,000 are believed to have died trying. Hundreds of thousands came to Canada.

These famine immigrants were the poorest of Ireland's poor, barely able to pay the £1 or £2 passage, unable to buy enough food to sustain themselves on the voyage over. Some had their tickets paid by landlords eager to evict them and be free of the taxes the English forced them to pay. Many Irish packed onto Canadian timber ships that otherwise would have made an empty and unprofitable return home to their Canadian port.

Of the Famine Irish, many didn't stay in Canada long, continuing on to the United States. Those who did stay supplied a pool of cheap labour that helped fuel Canada's economic expansion through the 1850s and 1860s. They erected bridges across the St. Lawrence into Montreal and heaved an industrialized nation into being.

Up until the massive wave of Famine Irish, Canada had plucked most of its immigrants from the preferred countries of England, Scotland and the United States. The Irish were Canada's first huge wave of "foreign" immigrants. And while they mostly spoke English, they didn't possess the religious, social or cultural tendencies of the British majority in Canada. It would mean years of suspicion and marginalization.

After the famine, the number of Irish immigrants to Canada decreased drastically. In the sixty years following the famine, between 1851 and 1910, 4,000,000 Irish left their homeland, compared with 2,000,000 during the five-year famine period. An estimated twenty percent of these emigrants went no further than Britain.

Overcoming Obstacles

The misery of the journey on board the coffin ships was only the first hurdle facing Irish immigrants coming to Canada. They were floating fever ships, thick with disease and filth. The religious divisions of the Irish homeland also followed the immigrants. The Protestant Irish and Catholic Irish were two distinct ethnic groups. The Catholics claimed themselves to be the original inhabitants of Ireland, colonized but never defeated by the British. The Protestants represented the Scottish and English colonists who came to Ireland under the rule of the British and who were often rewarded with free land for their loyalty to the Crown. The Irish Catholics and Protestants inherited a fierce mistrust of each other that, though often softened by individual acts of generosity, would take generations to heal in Canada.

The majority of Protestant Irish came to Canada with ample savings and a religious background that allowed them to fit in almost anywhere in British Canada. The Catholics, however, were socially and politically ghettoized in Ireland, and brought with them few advantages other than a familiarity with the English language, British institutions and the Catholic religion they shared with the French of Quebec. It wasn't nearly enough.

The Irish Catholics were English-speaking, which complicated their relations with the French. But it was Quebec that welcomed them most vigorously, partly because of religion and perhaps because of their shared resistance to the English. In the wake of their calamitous arrival at Grosse Ile, hundreds of Irish children were orphaned and alone. Quebec families and parishes rallied around these children, adopting them and allowing them to keep their Irish names. In Quebec today, fourth- and fifth-generation Donovans, O'Neills and O'Brians live as French-Canadians and do not speak English.

Outside Quebec, acceptance was more difficult. Irish Catholicism was frowned upon by the Protestant majority in other parts of Canada. And in Canada, citizenship was tied to the British Crown. Almost fanatical loyalty was practised as protection against American republicanism. Equally suspect was the Irish immigrant's rejection of farm labour. The cruelty of the famine years had turned them away from the land.

Canadian cities and towns quickly developed Irish sections or wards. These working-class neighbourhoods inflamed majority fears about social evils associated with American inner cities. The newcomers' Catholicism, their low wages, seasonal separation from their families and differences in their way of life made them painfully conspicuous as a minority group. But the Irish created a labour force ready and able to fill the seasonal employment demands of a newly expanded canal system, lumber industry and burgeoning railway network. Suspicions were hard to live down.

The Famine Irish had arrived poor and sick with cholera and typhus. The fear of spreading disease and of hungry, indigent hordes threatening public order worried government and public alike. The painful stereotype of the Irish Catholic as lazy, drunken and proliferate—the old hurts from home—followed them into English Canada and would remain etched in the public mind for several generations. It was a stereotype the Irish would defeat only through hard work, social ascendancy and education.

It was also difficult at times to be Irish and a good Catholic. The Fenian Brotherhood wanted to free Ireland by force of arms and was very popular among the Irish in the United States. In Canada the Fenians were considered seditious by the government, dangerous by the Protestants and an embarrassment by the Catholic church and respectable Catholic Irish. Fenian raids from the United States against British North America provoked anger toward Irish Catholics and solemn oaths of loyalty from the Catholic church. The Ancient Order of Hibernians was also dedicated, if less violently, to the cause of Irish nationalism, and fell afoul of the Catholic Church.

The Irish-Canadian Legacy

One advantage Protestant and Catholic Irish immigrants shared in coming to Canada was fluency, or at least some familiarity, with the English language. This allowed them to participate more immediately and more directly in Canadian society than many other non-English-speaking immigrants.

The social cohesiveness of Irish Catholics was of great benefit during their resettlement. Years of oppression had made the Irish very close-knit. They'd developed mutual aid societies to help one another. This independence of the state and natural generosity was underscored by a strong religious conviction that you were your brother's keeper. It was this kindness that helped soften a nation and made it more decent.

The Protestant Irish leaned toward the importance of the British connection in order to set themselves apart from their Catholic compatriots. The Orange Order, the original purpose of which in Ireland was to preserve British rule, at least in Ulster, was brought to Canada as a way for the Protestant Irish to win acceptance from their Scots and English neighbours. Individual Orange Order lodges existed in New Brunswick and in Upper Canada from the early part of the nineteenth century, and the order was consolidated in 1830 as the Grand Lodge of British North America. Whenever British institutions in Canada seemed threatened, Orangemen were fond of bringing up the Protestant victory over the Catholics at the River Boyne in 1690—a constant source of salt in an unhealed wound. The anniversary of that long-ago battle, July 12, remains the great Orange celebration.

For many years it was predominantly the Irish Catholics who supplied the working-class labour force necessary for the growth in communication, commerce and industry. But they were judged outsiders in a society and economy that was based on commerce and agriculture. Wealthy businessmen or homesteaders were supposedly the best kind of immigrants, not inner-city wage earners. Without farms or land, the Irish were perceived as rootless. It was a bias that would sting many other immigrants, but it was the Irish who were made to feel it first.

Today the descendants of Ireland's two ethnic immigrant groups make up more than ten percent of the Canadian population. Well-known Irish in Canada include:

Timothy Eaton, who emigrated to Canada in 1854 with £100 and in 1869 opened a little store on the southwest corner of Yonge and Queen, which became the foundation of a great retail organization serving all of Canada.

Nellie McClung, an activist and prominent campaigner in the drive for female suffrage in Manitoba and Alberta. McClung is a nationally known feminist and social reformer. Sixteen books and numerous articles made her one of Canada's best-known authors.

Francis Michael (King) Clancy grew up in Ottawa and went on to become a legend in the sport of hockey. King was a star defenceman in the National Hockey League, a coach, a referee and, finally, the vice-president of the Toronto Maple Leafs hockey club.

Other notables include John Joseph Lynch, D'Alton McCarthy, John O'Connor, Eugene O'Keefe, Michael Sullivan, Timothy Sullivan, Edmund Burke, Sir Guy Carleton, Benjamin Cronyn and Brian Mulroney, former leader of the Conservative Party and prime minister of Canada.

Perhaps the earliest Irish-Canadian statesman was Thomas D'Arcy McGee. First and foremost McGee was a champion of the rights of the Irish. He emigrated to the United States at the age of seventeen in 1842, but returned to his homeland during the famine years and led the fight for independence. In 1848, disguised as a priest, he made his way onto a ship bound for America.

From then on he was driven by the dominant concern of his life: the condition of the Irish in the United States and Canada. His efforts were directed through his pen; he circulated pamphlets and edited various newspapers. In 1857 he focused his attentions on Canada and made the transition from journalism to politics. McGee was elected as a Member of Parliament for Montreal and was instrumental in establishing the right of Catholics to funds for separate Catholic schools.

By this time, Father Bernard McGauran was continuing his own humanitarian efforts for the Irish. McGauran had survived the miserable summer of 1847 at Grosse Ile, despite his own bout with typhus. After his work was done for the Famine Irish, Father McGauran established St. Brigid's Home, a shelter for destitute Irish immigrants, widows and orphans. St. Brigid's still exists today as a senior citizen's residence and carries on with McGauran's legacy. The home has moved and grown over the years and now stands on a lot beside St. Patrick's cemetery, the burial place of Father Bernard McGauran.

Sources

1847, Grosse Ile: A Record of Daily Events, Andre Charbonneau and Andre Sevigny. Parks Canada, Ottawa, 1997.

Eyewitness: Grosse Isle 1847, Marianna O'Gallagher. Carraig Books, Quebec, 1995.

Famine Diary: Journey to a New World, Gerald Keegan and James J. Mangan. FSC; Wolfhound Press, Dublin, 1991.

The Fitzhenry & Whiteside Book of Canadian Facts & Dates, Jay Myers. Fitzhenry & Whiteside, Richmond Hill, 1991.

The Force of Hope, directed by Lindalee Tracey. White Pine Pictures, Toronto, 1998.

Grosse Ile, Gateway to Canada, 1832–1937, Marianna O'Gallagher. Carraig Books, Quebec, 1984.

Ocean Plague: The Diary of a Cabin Passenger, Robert Whyte, 1848.

The Irish in Canada, Volume I, Robert O'Driscoll and Lorna Reynolds, editors. Celtic Arts of Canada, Toronto, 1988.

The Irish Famine: An Illustrated History, Helen Litton. Wolfhound Press, Dublin, 1996.

Saint Brigid's, Québec, Marianna O'Gallagher. Carraig Books, Quebec, 1981.

A Short History of Ireland, Richard Killeen. Gill & Macmillan, Dublin, 1994.

The Untold Story: The Irish in Canada, Robert O'Driscoll and Lorna Reynolds, editors. Celtic Arts of Canada, Toronto, 1988.

The Voyage of the Naparima: The Diary of Gerald Keegan, James Mangan. Carraig Books, Quebec, 1982.

Mary Ann Shadd

Chapter Three
Breaking the Ice: Mary Ann Shadd

CANADA AND THE WORLD IN 1851

The Anti-Slavery Society of Canada is formed.

The first Canadian stamp, the three-penny black, is issued.

A telegraph line from Saint John to St. Andrew's is established.

The capital of Canada moves to Quebec City from Toronto.

The first North American YMCA is organized in Montreal.

American Isaac Singer invents the sewing machine.

Verdi writes the opera *Rigoletto*.

Herman Melville writes *Moby Dick*.

Ready-made ice-cream, safety pins and coal stoves became widely available in the 1850s.

The morning was hushed and green as Mary Ann moved through Chatham on her stretched out Sunday legs. Black legs, black woman, mind roaming free in Canada West. Savouring itself.

Mary Ann stopped hard at the white men bunched on the street. Something was squirming between them—a shoeless black child trying to get free. Memory hardened like bone—100 years of chains jangled, 100,000 voices groaned. The white men were slavers.

Lunging, Mary Ann tore the boy away and raced to the courthouse, ringing the bell so furiously that the whole town raised up its head. The American slave-hunters had committed an outrage against the British flag, she told them with that steady gaze she had. The town jeered with indignation and chased the slavers out. But they'd be back—the American Fugitive Slave Bill sent too many white hands reaching into Canada to grab blacks back into slavery. After five years up north, Mary Ann Shadd was still trying to stop them.

Mary Ann had come to Canada to educate black minds and white. She was unflinching in her determination to emancipate and integrate American blacks on both sides of the border. She had learned her fierceness back home in the United States.

Mary Ann was born in Wilmington, Delaware, in 1823, the first of thirteen children. She was mulatto coloured, her skin lightened by a German great-grandfather who had fallen in love with a black woman during the Seven Years War. Their children and their children's children were free-born—a precarious privilege in the slave state of Delaware. Mary Ann grew up loved and encouraged to think. Her father, Abraham, was a shoemaker and a conductor on the Underground Railroad, helping escaped slaves. The Shadd home was a safe house and Abraham risked his life with every generous act.

These were slavery times, when black existence was fortified by a single word: courage. Courage in the white face of brute force, in the theft of one's own children, courage to endure a century of silence. Mary Ann learned duty deeply, growing up in the fearful whispers of escaping slaves and in the steady thud of their bare feet moving past her house. Her mother fed them, her father hid them and sometimes gave them shoes. The slaves had come up from hell, the monstrous plantations of the deep south where lashed, black backs held up the cotton industry. They were heading north, to "free states" like Ohio, Illinois and Michigan. Canada wasn't yet a favoured destination, though vague rumours had reached the Shadd family. It was somewhere at the tail end of the North Star, through the dark and frozen unknown. George W. Clarke, an American abolitionist, penned these words:

I'm on my way to Canada
That cold and distant land
The dire effects of slavery
I can no longer stand—
Farewell, old master,
Don't come after me
I'm on my way to Canada
Where coloured men are free.

Blacks had been trying to get to Canada since the late 1700s, often helped by white Quakers. By the turn of that century there were over forty black settlements in British North America. But slavery had also been legal in Canada. One thousand slaves were living in New France when the British conquered Quebec in 1759. When Loyalists fled the American Revolution, they brought 2,000 more slaves into Canada; when black Loyalists fled, they brought their belief in British justice. Sometimes it wasn't deserved.

John Graves Simcoe, lieutenant-governor, had passed the Upper Canada Abolition Act in 1793, limiting slavery and promising gradual emancipation. It was the first legislation against slavery in the British Empire. The same year the United States Congress passed its first Fugitive Slave Law. Escaped slaves could now be dragged back from free states within the American union. Black status was reconfirmed—men, women and children were property.

Back and forth they moved across the border, black families looking for a home, often used as pawns in the great colonial slicing up. The British offered emancipation and land in Canada if blacks would fight in the Revolutionary War. Later the Union would offer them freedom as a knife to the throat of the southern Confederacy.

Word wound through the south about Canada's miracles—black Loyalists and free men fighting side by side with white Canadians during the War of 1812, the abolition of slavery in 1834. Canada lodged in the black imagination, despite the propaganda of slave-owners who warned of its desolate cold and native cannibals. Canada was a terrible contradiction, both succoring and devouring.

Mary Ann often heard her Abraham talk of emigration to Africa, Jamaica, even north on the "Canadian Venture"—but as a last resort. He'd raised his family proud, on notions of reason and good manners. Blacks could earn their freedom through due process and education. But the law was tightening like a noose and privileges were shrinking, even for free blacks. Preacher Nat Turner led a slave revolt in 1831, butchering his master and fifty-four other whites in Virginia. The whole South shuddered, retaliating with harsher slave codes. Free blacks and slaves whispered more emphatically about emigration, and a wobbly abolition movement got started. Anti-slavery newspapers began printing words that had rarely been spoken out loud. Their white publishers were tarred and feathered, sometimes killed. Mary Ann's father defied caution, writing and selling the abolitionist *Liberator*. Many states forbade free blacks from even reading it on pain of twenty-five lashes.

But something fierce was coming alive in black America, something big and hopeful. In 1833 Mary Ann's father joined the National Convention for the Improvement of Free People of Colour. They talked and talked about emigration and education; about preparing the way for freedom. Abraham moved his family to Pennsylvania so his children could be educated. Delaware was still a slave state—there were no separate schools for blacks and no chance they'd be allowed to sit in white ones.

For six years Mary Ann studied at a Quaker-run school, a rare privilege for a black child. She was ten then, hungry to learn, bent into her studies with the squinting intensity of an adult. She decided to become a teacher. Mary Ann brought her learning back to Wilmington, leaving only when it opened a separate black school. Then she roamed, teaching all over and filling up her mind.

Mary Ann fed on the new intellectual mood of the 1840s, ear bent to the talk of the time, to the great thinkers debating the God-given essentials of liberty. Whites and free blacks coalesced into congresses to map the dream of freedom. Mary Ann came into herself in this decade, piecing together a philosophy of hard work, self-reliance and integration. She learned by example that all colours *could* work together. She entered the circle of the new black intelligentsia: Martin Delaney, the first black graduate at Harvard, and Frederick Douglass, the former slave and self-taught publisher of *North Star*. In 1849 she began writing articles for the *Douglass's Paper*. In the background of these times abolitionists' children rhymed off the "anti-slavery alphabet":

U is for Upper Canada,
where the poor slave has found
rest after all his wanderings
for it is British ground.

Then hope failed. In 1850 the second Fugitive Slave Bill was enacted and legislation grabbed back abolition advances. No black was safe, not even the free-born Shadds. Anyone could be hauled off by any white claiming her as property. Thousands of slaves scrambled toward Canada on the Underground Railroad, travelling by the light of the North Star, by rumour and deep-down instinct. They reached for the safety of the British "lion's paw."

Canada rallied, puffing up with moral superiority after so many crouching years in America's shadow. It was an idea that would forever shape national identity:

Canada the good and America the evil. Mary Ann thought the mass exodus might bring trouble. A sudden, unschooled population of freed black slaves would need a tight grip on self-worth. First freedoms would have to be tasted responsibly to avoid the backlash of disapproving whites. Blacks would not be allowed to fail, could not, if they wanted to live down the stigma of inferiority and inspire the abolition movement. America was watching.

In 1851 Mary Ann and her brother Isaac came north on the "Canadian Venture" to help educate refugees. She was twenty-eight years old, fixed in her life's calling. She and Isaac landed in Toronto for the first North American Convention of Coloured Freemen. All the big star abolitionists were there, talking freedom and strategies, setting Mary Ann's mind on fire, making her feel at home. She met Henry Bibb and his wife, Mary, escaped slaves who'd landed in Windsor and published *The Voice of the Fugitive*. They told her that Windsor needed black teachers. That's all Mary Ann needed to hear. Isaac stayed in Toronto while Mary Ann rushed to Windsor, crashing into a philosophical divide that would nearly crush her. But she started out hopeful, dashing off a cautionary note to another brother in Buffalo: "I have been here more than a week and like Canada. I do not feel prejudice....If you come, be particular about company. If boarding go where white and coloured board. Every man is respected and patronized according to his ability, capacity and the respectable stand he takes."

Windsor was a smidgen of a place, fast swelling with penniless black refugees streaming in from Detroit. "This is by universal consent, the most destitute community of colored people, known in this province...." Mary Ann wrote. An eyesore. Whites were welcoming but Mary Ann knew their generosity wasn't infinite. Already both communities were retreating into suspiciousness. It wasn't so much malice as ignorance, she reckoned; blacks and whites had no practice living together equally. Hate was an acquired impulse, called upon in times of doubt. Integrated education was one of the only tools to bring minds together.

But the Common Schools Act had legally segregated public education in Canada West the year before, in 1851. There was no place for blacks to learn except privately. The Bibbs wanted a segregated school; Mary Ann insisted on an integrated one. It was an idea before its time; a shock to public sentiment. Blacks and whites were skittish.

In September Mary Ann Shadd took a big gulp, straightened her hair and opened her integrated private school in an abandoned army building. Students of both colours arrived, children in the day, adults at night. Mary Ann charged fifty cents a month tuition, but money was so scarce that parents sometimes paid in wood or not at all. Mary Ann agonized over funding to keep classes going. Worse, she had provoked the ire of the Bibbs. Rumours began to swirl around Mary Ann, conjured mostly by her former friends. It was a rivalry for leadership—Henry Bibb had been the single voice of the black community before Mary Ann arrived. Stubborn, know-it-all, Mary Ann.

Mary Ann figured it differently. She saw Henry Bibb trading on the myth of the broken-down slave, the man-child, wobbling in his freedom. His newspaper was full of grim reports on black destitution, appeals to white pity and charity. Mary Ann loathed it. What the world needed to see was the hard-working black, the citizen. The needy black was the scourge of opportunity, the pronouncement of failure. That whites fell for it made Mary Ann suspicious of their generosity. That blacks like Bibb perpetuated it made her ashamed.

Mary Ann elbowed her way through that first year and into the next, teaching day and night. Some of the students were so eager to learn after the blankness of slavery, but others dropped in and out of class, unused to regularity, or scared off by their teacher's radical reputation. Mary Ann was bewildered and so frustrated by their apathy she complained to her old teacher. Mrs. Kirby wrote her back:

> Dearest: I dare say the condition of the world looks hopeless enough to you on whom the burden of wrong peculiarly presses, and yet, dear, the seed is germinating. The printed and spoken word is never lost. It bears perfect fruit in due season. You must indeed work in faith, dear. The coming years will assure you, such labours as yours began at the very root of the tree. Dear, it is my opinion that the colored race is the most elastic and teachable people on the earth and before a century has elapsed, this people will give more.

But the black community grew suspicious of Mary Ann—Bibb kept smearing her in his newspaper, accusing her of unwomanly hard-headedness and of shoddy financial accounting. He hinted she was less than a model Christian for refusing to attend all-black churches—Mary Ann preferred integrated ones. The slander cut off funds from the American Missionary Association and in 1853 Mary Ann's school had to close. Another one wouldn't open until 1862. And integrated education wouldn't come to Windsor until 1888.

It was a relief for Mary Ann when her parents finally moved up to Windsor, a safe home to curl into and to be understood. But there was little stillness for Mary Ann's mind; thoughts whirred about blacks left behind, the ones who'd grown afraid on their white masters' stories. Mary Ann began working on a small book. *A Plea for Emigration, Or, Notes of Canada West* was a primer on Canada for escaping slaves: "In Canada, as in other recently settled countries, there is much to do....If a coloured man understands his business, he receives the public patronage the same as a white man. He is not obliged to work a little better, and at a lower rate...every man's work stands or falls according to merit, not as is his colour."

Mary Ann was rigourous in her research and rosy in her outlook, detailing climate and crops, jobs, schools, religions, cultural and business practices. She wrote about self-sufficiency and frugality, emphasizing the importance of black character and integration. Real freedom meant living beyond the confines of "blackness," she argued. Fugitives had to learn to move among white people, just as whites had to learn to live among them. They had to succeed outside their own communities, otherwise they'd be condemned to ghettos, forever measured as separate and inferior. Of course, Mary Ann had experienced the better side of whites, and had grown up expecting equality.

It was these abstract ideas that separated Mary Ann from her own people—white-schooled Mary Ann, as foreign to illiterate slaves as freedom, their future self. And yet she was understood instinctively, known deep down inside them, beneath the hate and hurt. Mary Ann appealed to their survival, demanded that they flourish. But she'd never been enslaved, her ideas were free-born, not burned into raw flesh. Her free legs had carried her into places, lifted her up to a wider view. It might have been the fundamental difference between her and Henry Bibb, a freed slave who carried the wounds of indignity and the furious certainty of a debt owed. He had learned to beg from white men and perhaps to hate them for it. Mary Ann had not.

A Plea for Emigration spread through the United States and Canada, confirming Mary Ann as a black leader and abolitionist. Henry Bibb must have gone hard with envy. He chided Mary Ann for printing her book in the United States. Mary Ann hit back with a newspaper of her own.

In March of 1853 the *Provincial Freeman* was launched, making Mary Ann Shadd the first black woman publisher in North America. Maybe the world. She hid behind the credibility of Reverend Samuel Ringgold Ward—women weren't supposed to run newspapers. Readers could now choose between two points of view: Shadd's integration and Bibb's segregation. Both papers featured local news, events and editorials, and news from American abolitionists. But venom continued to spill out of Henry Bibb. In 1854 Mary Ann moved her headquarters to Toronto to put a little distance between them.

The times were small-minded. Mary Ann had to navigate around gender as much as race, sharpening her mind and manners like weapons. She worked feverishly, writing editorials and raising money to keep things going—spinster work, some might say, for an unmarried thirty-three-year-old woman. Then Thomas Cary got hold of her heart. Thomas owned a Toronto barbershop and supplied the city with ice. He was a leader in the abolition movement and raised money for the *Provincial Freeman*. Cary wasn't scared off by a hard-headed newspaperwoman. But readers didn't know that editor M. A. Shadd was a woman; they didn't have the imagination to guess. When Mary Ann printed the truth, their shoulders turned colder than Thomas's ice. Mary Ann moved the paper to Chatham. And she got a new name.

In 1856 Mary Ann married Thomas; "Mrs. Cary" had a ring of respectability. But the bride and groom didn't even live in the same city, not that Mary Ann cared what kind of scandal that caused. She was travelling to the States a lot, signing up readers and rallying abolition forces. Trying to keep clear of the rabid dog of a Fugitive Bill that was still chasing down blacks. In 1857, Mary Ann's first baby was born: Sarah Elizabeth Cary. Motherhood didn't keep her home much, either; too many people needed saving.

All through the 1850s abolitionists zigzagged across the border, trying to rescue slaves and bring them north. Some say as many as 500 Canadian blacks made the trip each year. Harriet Tubman settled in St. Catharines and freed 300 slaves on nineteen trips south. In 1858, the most famous white anti-slaver stole across the border into Chatham. John Brown had plans to raid a federal arsenal in Kansas and then to attack plantations with a guerrilla army and set slaves free. Mary Ann let him use her printing press and office. Forty-six people showed up for Brown's secret meeting, including Mary Ann and Thomas, her brother Isaac and their *Freeman* reporter, Osborne Anderson. Brown picked a provisional government from the crowd, then quietly returned to the United States to plot his raid on Harpers Ferry. History was moving fast.

On April 12, 1859, shots rang out at Fort Sumter in Charleston, South Carolina, and the Civil War began. Canadian blacks held back their hope; it wasn't a war about freedom yet. Four more years would pass before Abraham Lincoln would issue a decree freeing slaves. Blacks still pinned their hearts to Canada, working to sturdy their futures here. Abraham Shadd was elected to a seat on the Raleigh Town Council, the first black to hold elected office in British North America. It was a remarkable victory, but not a whole one. Every black knew that only a few hundred miles south, family and friends remained chained. They waited for news from America.

In October of 1859, John Brown made his famous raid on Harpers Ferry and Colonel Robert E. Lee stomped it dead. Twenty-one accomplices were routed and only a single black man escaped. Osborne Anderson, Mary Ann's reporter for *Provincial Freeman,* scrambled back to Canada. John Brown was hanged on December 9 and black hope dangled with him. But his memory didn't fade for many generations:

John Brown's body lies a-mouldering in the grave,
But his soul goes marching on.

It was a season for endings, a closing-down time. Mary Ann wrote her last editorial about Harpers Ferry and within a few months, the *Provincial Freeman* folded. A year later Thomas Cary died. They'd had only five years together, five interrupted and abbreviated years lived along the border's edge of duty. Somewhere there might have been a sunset for two old lovers to love—gone now. Mary Ann was a widow. Five months later she gave birth to a boy she called Linton. Mary Ann became a single mother of two small children.

In 1862 Mary Ann Cary became a naturalized Canadian citizen. But a part of her was already leaving. The Civil War was finally dividing along race lines and abolitionists were gaining ground. On January 1, 1863, President Lincoln issued a decree freeing all slaves in states then in rebellion against the Union. The Emancipation Proclamation pierced every black heart with these long-lived-for words "all persons held as slaves...are, and henceforward, shall be free."

Shall be free.

And while absolute freedom wouldn't come until the defeat of the Confederacy and the passage of the Thirteenth Amendment of the constitution, it was enough for blacks to hurry back. Thirty-five thousand Canadians joined the Union army, black and white. Every able-bodied black man in Abraham Shadd's new home of Buxton signed up. Their presence in Canada dwindled. The "Canadian Venture" was ending.

Mary Ann couldn't stop the pull on her own heart either. The Governor of Indiana, Levi P. Morton, wanted to appoint her to recruit blacks for the Union side. Mary Ann accepted the commission, becoming one of the few, if not only, paid women recruitment agents in the United States. But her idealism had its pragmatic side. Mary Ann got a Canadian passport, perhaps to ensure British protection if she ever needed it.

Her assignment took her all over the States during the last years of the Civil War. After it was over she settled in Washington, D.C., and was principal of several large public schools for seventeen years. While she taught in the day, she studied law at night, at Howard University, the newly opened black school. She completed her studies in 1872 but wasn't allowed a degree because she was a woman. It was a ridiculous irony for a woman who'd broken the very ground upon which black universities existed, who had schooled so many black minds open. Finally, she was called to the bar in 1881 at the age of fifty-eight. A year later her beloved father, Abraham, died in Buxton, Ontario.

Mary Ann never did come back to live in Canada, but her footprints remained, marking the path of a single woman's courage and of a people's freedom. After twelve feisty years of living in Canada, Mary Ann left many of her family here. Her brother Alfred taught at Buxton Mission School; sister Emaline graduated first in her class at Toronto Normal School, and then taught in Kent County. Garrison became a wealthy farmer, while Isaac, who had accompanied Mary Ann north that first summer in 1851, returned south to enter politics.

Mary Ann Shadd died in Washington on June 5, 1893; a hard-headed woman and abolitionist who forced a new nation to consider the true meaning of freedom. Emancipation from slavery meant little without full citizenship, equal education and personal responsibility. It was the free mind, able to think intelligently and to choose, that was the hallmark of inclusion. While the last segregated school closed in Ontario in 1965, Mary Ann's example opened school doors to black students and white all through the twentieth century, especially in the smaller towns and cities. The faces of children in classrooms today bear the casual nonchalance of inclusion, a right that Mary Ann Shadd won for them over a century before.

Black Immigration History in Canada

In 1851 Mary Ann Shadd fled the United States as part of the confident, educated mainstream. She was a free-born black woman in a time when most of her people were in chains. Though black people had lived in Canada long before Mary Ann, very few had arrived directly from their ancestral homeland in the continent of Africa.

Olivier Le Jeune was the first slave to be brought directly from Africa to Canada. He was sold in Quebec in 1629, but died a free man. By 1759, New France recorded 3,604, many of whom were native; 1,132 were black. Most of them lived in or near Montreal and worked as domestic servants. Because the early economy was small and didn't rely on a single crop or mass production and gang labour, slavery didn't develop among the French colonists. But later British colonists reintroduced it. The United Empire Loyalists brought about 2,000 black slaves with them into British North America, mostly to the Maritimes.

Between 1763 and 1865, most blacks migrating to Canada were fleeing the shackles of American slavery. When the American colonies won independence from Britain in 1783, blacks who had sided with the Loyalists fled the United States for the safety of British territory. A small number moved to Upper Canada, which later became the province of Ontario, but by far the largest number, approximately 3,500, settled in the Maritimes, particularly in Nova Scotia. In 1796 a band of Jamaican Maroons also headed north. Descendants of black slaves who had escaped from the Spanish and later the British rulers of Jamaica, the Maroons were feared and respected for their courage.

Canada became fixed in the black imagination as a land of freedom, largely for its early stand on slavery. In 1793 Governor John Simcoe challenged the legality of slavery in Upper Canada, making it the only colony to legislate for the abolition of slavery. It was a gradual emancipation—that new slaves could no longer be bought or sold, but blacks already enslaved remained the property of their owners. By 1800, courts in other parts of British North America had moved to eliminate slavery and in August 1833 the British Parliament passed a law abolishing slavery in all the colonies. The law went into effect August of 1834. For American blacks, Britain became their protector. And they showed astonishing loyalty.

During the War of 1812, nearly 2,000 black immigrants came to Canada, siding with the British over the Americans. These immigrants were lured by promises that their loyalty would be rewarded with freedom and land grants. In fact, the land was often poor, if it existed at all. Some refugees had to wait until as late as the 1840s for their land.

The largest number of American blacks arrived in Canada independent of any promises. They came along a network of secret routes known as the Underground Railroad, the rescue effort that started operating in the 1780s. It's estimated that by the end of the American Civil War as many as 30,000 slaves had escaped along the Underground Railroad to find freedom in Canada. This included about 800 free African-Americans who migrated from California to Vancouver Island in the late 1850s hoping to escape discriminatory laws in their home state.

When American slavery ended in 1865, thousands of Canadian blacks returned to the United States. But other blacks continued to arrive in small numbers over the next century, mostly because of inequalities in the U.S. More than 1,000 left Oklahoma to settle on the Canadian prairies, particularly Alberta between 1909 and 1911. The United States remained the main source of new black immigrants until the later part of the twentieth century.

The black population in Canada didn't grow much until the 1960s, when changes to the Immigration Act allowed large numbers of West Indians and Africans into Canada. This wave of black immigrants greatly outnumbered the original black population in every Canadian region except the Maritimes. Between 1950 and 1995 about 300,000 immigrants from the West Indies and over 150,000 from Africa, including people of Asian and European descent, arrived. Today African-Canadians constitute about two percent of the Canadian population.

Overcoming Obstacles

While many white Canadians morally opposed slavery and helped escaping slaves from the United States, others feared their arrival, seeing them as backward, immoral and criminal, as well as an economic threat. Blacks were treated primarily as a source of cheap labour and poverty stood in their way as much as other people's ignorance. Even after the final abolition of slavery throughout the British Empire in 1884, blacks faced a great deal of social prejudice.

Discrimination had existed from the very beginning of black migration into Canada, and with it, ideas of segregation. Blacks were scattered across the country, and away from whites.

Government policies insured that most black Loyalists, Maroons and refugees in the Maritimes were sent to segregated communities on the outskirts of larger white towns. In Quebec, many of the slaves owned by white Loyalists were sent to live in the Eastern Townships. All-black communities developed around Halifax, Shelburne, Digby and Guysborough in Nova Scotia, and Saint John and Fredericton in New Brunswick.

In Ontario, fleeing slaves from the Underground Railroad also tended to settle in segregated communities, but more for mutual support and protection against a white Canadian population that wasn't always welcoming and American bounty-hunters who were intrepid. Most of Ontario's blacks settled around Windsor, Chatham, London, St. Catharines and Hamilton. Toronto had a black district, and there were smaller concentrations of blacks near Barrie, Owen Sound and Guelph. Saltspring Island and the city of Victoria were the main locations for black settlers in nineteenth-century British Columbia. Early twentieth-century migrants to Alberta established several rural communities around Edmonton.

Canada's black population was relatively isolated not only from whites but from each other. The pattern broke down in the 1930s and '40s when rural blacks began migrating to the cities in search of jobs. Many of the original black settlements were abandoned or considerably depopulated.

Early black Loyalists and Maroons had difficulty establishing themselves in the Maritimes. The small land grants they received weren't enough to make a living on. Forced to seek work in neighbouring white towns, the blacks were often exploited and badly paid. Poverty was a relentless obstacle facing early black pioneers. In 1792, many early black immigrants left Nova Scotia and New Brunswick for Sierra Leone in West Africa, when almost 1,200 black Loyalists sailed from Halifax to found the new settlement of Freetown. Their descendants can still be identified there today. Eight years later, another 500 Maroons followed the same route to Sierra Leone. They arrived during a black Loyalist rebellion against their British governors. By siding with the colonial authorities, the Maroons ensured the failure of the rebellion. Again in 1820, black refugees picked up and left. Ninety-five blacks steamed out of Halifax for Trinidad.

The fugitive blacks who had arrived in Ontario via the Underground Railroad were almost always destitute. Without the cushion of government land grants, they were forced to become labourers on other people's farms, although some farmed their own land successfully, and some worked for the Great Western Railway. Many of those who went to Victoria, B.C., in the 1850s brought skills or savings that helped them start up small businesses. They worked on farms or in shops on the new wharf at Esquimalt, B.C. But until well into the twentieth century, most African-Canadians were employed in the lower-paying service categories or as unskilled labourers.

The Black-Canadian Legacy

While often marginalized by geography, their concentrated settlements allowed blacks to retain their distinct cultural identity and create a close-knit, self-sufficient community. The main institution of support was the church, usually Baptist or Methodist, which came into being because white congregations often refused blacks as members. The church not only played a spiritual role, but a major social and political one within the black community. In the twentieth century the churches led the movement for greater educational opportunity and civil rights.

Black women offered another remarkable legacy to their community and their adopted country. Slavery had forced them to work to support themselves, and circumstances perpetuated this tradition in Canada. Black women have always played an important economic role in family life and have experienced considerable independence as a result. Raised in a communal fashion, frequently by their grandparents or older neighbours, black children developed family-like relationships throughout the local community. A strong sense of group identity and mutual reliance, combined with the unique identity provided by the churches, produced an intimate community life and a refuge against white discrimination.

From the very beginning of their settlement in Canada, blacks expressed an intense loyalty to Britain and Canada. Black Loyalists fought to maintain British rule in America, and their awareness that an American invasion could mean their re-enslavement prompted them to participate in Canada's defence. Black militiamen fought against American troops in the War of 1812, and were prominent in subduing the Rebellions of 1837 and the Fenian raids. In the 1860s the largely self-financed black Pioneer Rifle Corps was the only armed force protecting Vancouver Island, although later it was denied participation in the Vancouver Island Volunteer Rifle Corps. During WW I recruitment offices initially rejected blacks, but persistent volunteering led to the formation of a separate black corps, the Nova Scotia Number Two Construction Battalion.

Blacks have also been active in every political party since Confederation. Black municipal councillors and school trustees have been common for more than a century, notably Mifflin Gibbs, who sat on the Victoria City Council in the 1860s and was a delegate to the Yale Convention, which considered B.C.'s entry into Confederation, and William Hubbard, who served as councillor, controller and acting mayor of Toronto 1894 to 1907.

Leonard Braithwaite became the first African-Canadian in a provincial legislature when he was elected in Ontario in 1963, and Lincoln Alexander from Hamilton became the first black federal member in 1968. Emery Barnes and Rosemary Brown were both elected in the 1970s to the B.C. legislature. New honours were achieved in the 1980s when Lincoln Alexander became lieutenant-governor of Ontario, Alvin Curling joined the Ontario cabinet, Anne Cools was appointed to the Senate and Howard McCurdy of Windsor, Ontario, was elected to the House of Commons. In 1990 Donald Oliver of Halifax joined the Senate and Zanana Akande became a member of the Ontario cabinet, the first black woman to achieve that rank in Canada. In 1993 Wayne Adams entered the Nova Scotia cabinet and in the federal election that year three black MPs were elected: Jean Augustine, Hedy Fry and Ovid Jackson. Hedy Fry, from Vancouver, was appointed to the cabinet in 1996.

Sources

The Black Canadians, Their History and Contribution, Velma Carter and Levero Carter. Readmore Books, Edmonton, 1989.

The Blacks in Canada, Robin Winks. McGill-Queen's University Press, Montreal, 1971.

Breaking the Ice: The Story of Mary Ann Shadd, directed by Sylvia Sweeney. White Pine Pictures, Toronto, 1998.

The Fitzhenry & Whiteside Book of Canadian Facts & Dates, Jay Myers. Fitzhenry & Whiteside, Richmond Hill, 1991.

The Freedom Seekers: Blacks in Early Canada, Daniel G. Hill. The Book Society of Canada, Toronto, 1981.

Mary Ann Shadd: Publisher, Editor, Teacher, Lawyer, Suffragette, Rosemary Sadlier. Umbrella Press, Toronto, 1995.

A Plea for Emigration, Or, Notes of Canada West, Mary A. Shadd. Mercury Press, Toronto, 1998.

Shadd: The Life and Times of Mary Ann Shadd Cary, Jim Bearden and Linda Jean Butler. New Canada Publications, Toronto, 1977.

Slaves, Stan Persky. New Star Books, Vancouver, 1974.

T. Phillips Thompson

Chapter Four
An English Sense of Justice: T. Phillips Thompson

Canada and the World in 1857

A bill is passed to put Canada on the decimal (dollar) system of currency.

The Canadian Rifles Regiment is sent to the Red River to ward off American influence.

The steamer *Montreal* sinks near Quebec, killing 253 people, mostly immigrants.

The first attempt to lay an Atlantic telegraph cable from Ireland to Trinity Bay, Newfoundland, fails.

Queen Victoria chooses Ottawa as the new capital.

Nova Scotia is the first province to offer education to the hearing- and speech-impaired.

American E.G. Otis installs the first safety elevator.

Cattle disease is widespread in Europe.

Indian sepoys mutiny against British rule.

The Irish Republican Brotherhood, the Fenians, is founded in New York.

Postage stamps, rubberized raincoats, coal furnaces and inexpensive pocket watches become widely available in the 1850s.

Tom Phillips Thompson looked ancient as Moses in his eighties, the grand old man whom cub reporters made yearly pilgrimages to. Half-blind, snowy-bearded Thompson had outlived his century and was revered. He sat at his rolltop desk in Oakville, Ontario, still roiling against political hypocrisy and the one-legged pace of social justice, exasperated at the persistence of human greed.

In those last years he sometimes nestled beneath his apple trees, his mind rubbing against itself like a finger on polished stone. Feeling for the gouges of history, the long-dead names of half-lost causes—Louis Riel's Métis, the Knights of Labour, the vote for women, Free Trade, Canada First—his mind unwinding in the shape of a nation. Sometimes Thompson's chin drooped and he'd fall asleep, dreaming of his beginning again, among the smokestacks of northern England.

Newcastle-upon-Tyne always wheezed in Thompson's thoughts, a grimy foundry town stoked by the industrial revolution and the brute fact of class. He was born there in 1843, the second son of Quakers. Even his memories hurried away from the place. He'd seen whole families fed to the factories, children too. He'd watched his father, William, go bankrupt twice, losing his grocery because of the credit he gave too freely to the working men. The penalty for kindness was sinking below your class. From very early, Tom Phillips was suspicious of capitalism and of caste privilege.

Tom Phillips Thompson was fourteen when his family set out for the Province of Canada. They settled in St. Catharines, Canada West, where his father opened a real estate office. A few years later, Tom Phillips studied law, then worked for his father as an insurance inspector. Around him, a nation was rising, as well as the quarrels of nation builders. The capital, having hopscotched across Canada East and West, had been firmly decided on by Queen Victoria as Ottawa, in 1858.

Queen Victoria!

Canada had surprised Tom Phillips; such a British place in such a British century, he thought, still bullied by the empire's lords and officers and second sons, curtseying madly in pursuit of itself. He'd heard the arguments about confederation spreading across the colony—minds pondering American-style republicanism and British parliamentarianism. He was twenty-one when he published his own opinion in an 1864 manifesto. Called "The Future Government of Canada," it took a whack at the country that had ruined his father:

> The time must come for Canada to cease her present connection with the British Empire....Canada can exist as an independent nation...not a monarchy or aristocracy....What could be more ridiculous than to bestow class privileges...because of the achievement of some ancestor. Remove class distinction and bestow on all the same advantages, regardless of race, creed, colour or condition. Give all...a fair start in the race of life....This is the 19th century...the age of progress.

It was a raw, intemperate cry of idealism—the mind's first freedom to proclaim itself. Young men went to war and died for such grand thoughts. His position had been daring, but small-minded, too. While he'd decried British imperialism, Tom Phillips had also demanded a homogeneous nation where the French of Canada East would be forced to assimilate. It was a position he'd later regret.

His manifesto had given Tom Phillips an appetite for writing. He liked the order it imposed on his own disparate thoughts. Two years later, he landed his first writing job on the *St. Catharines Post,* reporting on the Fenian Raids. A group of Irish-Americans aided by Civil War vets, the Fenians were agitating for a national uprising in Ireland. Part of the plan was to invade Canada as a way of securing Irish independence from England. Fenians had already been defeated in New Brunswick in April 1866. On June 1, another group crossed Niagara, overtaking Canadian militiamen at Ridgeway; the next day more Fenians moved into Missisquoi Bay, Quebec. They were soon routed and, failing to inspire the hoped-for Irish uprising, quickly fell apart. But their effect in Canada was profound; by providing an external threat, they helped unite Canadians on the eve of Confederation.

Growing confident in his skills, Tom Phillips headed for Toronto, getting a job at the *Daily Telegraph,* on the police court beat. He distinguished himself by mastering the slouched vernacular of the lower classes. There was lots to write about: wife-beaters, drunks and the down-and-outs on vagrancy charges. It was a sin and a crime to be poor; perhaps it still was—people went to jail for having no visible means of support. Tom Phillips wasn't concerned about that; he was writing a humorous column:

"Ann Nolan, a bloated looking female, who appeared to be fast approaching spontaneous combustion, was charged with being found lying asleep on Spadina

Avenue last night, her sole companion being a black bottle, the contents of which had been partially demolished."

"Michael Conner, a tough old seed was destitute of capillary substances on the summit of his cranium...fell a victim to the intoxicating cup."

"Eliza Wise, a foolish virgin, was brought up for disorderly conduct. Wise by name but not by thinking. The prisoner was removed and...kicked viciously and interspersed the proceedings by loud screams and curses."

Later he would wince, remembering how he'd poked fun at the poor—it was a cruel thing to have done. But at the time his satire *was* getting noticed. Tom Phillips was invited to work at the more prestigious *Mail* in 1870, and became a minor celebrity. He wrote his column under the nom de plume "Jimuel Briggs, D.B. (Dead Beat), recently graduated from the mythical but esteemed Coboconk University." Briggs, was a bumbling Inspector Clouseau-like reporter who stumbled onto political corruption, patronage deals and hypocrisies. Readers loved it.

While Tom Phillips sharpened his political satire at the *Mail,* young Delia Fischer from Guelph was submitting turgid poetry: "I cannot rest yet night is near / Calm night! When even care is hushed / Yet who can rest when love is near / Or who can sleep whom love has cursed."

Perhaps Tom Phillips met Delia through the newspaper, or on one of her trips to Toronto. She was bright, beautiful, curious and, as one of twelve daughters, particularly marriageable. In 1872, he proposed. He was twenty-eight. Delia recorded their life in her diary: "April 28, 1872: I am married now. I sit for hours alone staring at that magic ring....I only for health & love in the end." A year later, little Clara Florence was born, the first of the Thompsons' five children.

Tom Phillips was doing well, climbing into the establishment, or at least being read by them; claiming his rightful British place at the top of the heap of an immigrant nation. He could have kept building on his celebrity, on his talent for insightful political commentary, but something gnawed at his conscience. Maybe he grew bored entertaining the establishment, or embarrassed. The political bias of the dailies was so strong that they didn't even cover the other side in election campaigns. And whole constituencies were being ignored by the press—farmers and working people barely existed. Tom Phillips started to question his profession, and his place in it, influenced, perhaps, by the emergence of a vocal working class.

Workers in Ontario and Quebec began rallying behind the nine-hour workday movement in 1872. In Hamilton, 1,500 of them paraded through the streets in May, while in Toronto, printers went on strike against George Brown's *Globe*. It was the kind of labour muscle that scared the establishment and that had been kept illegal. But the Toronto strike forced Prime Minister John A. Macdonald to introduce the Trade Unions Act, which, for the first time, made unions legal, not illegal conspiracies. A new and legitimized voice was added to the national chorus.

Tom Phillips quit the *Mail* and joined forces with Henry Smallpiece, a local publisher. Together they launched *The National*, a weekly newspaper of political commentary that set out to serve the interests of the farmers and workers. "*The National* will be bound by no slavish deference to English or American models....Our journal shall be an independent one...and neither party, monetary or social influences shall render it otherwise." It was a rare promise.

The National began with the tag line "Canada First," a show of support for the new movement attacking the elitism of Confederation. Canada First was a nationalist group demanding representation for all Canadians and separation from U.S. influence. But to do that, they were willing to retain some connection to Britain. Worse, they had an Ontario bias that helped fan hatred against French and Catholics and, later, the Métis rebellion. Tom Phillips eventually realized they were just another clubby bunch of privileged white guys. He changed the paper's tag line to "Judicious But Effectual Protection to Native Industry." America remained a threat and Tom Phillips's editorials warned that free trade would keep Canadian farmers impoverished. But something worse had already arrived.

Tom Phillips hadn't really noticed the poor until they started hovering in the doorways of Toronto and their children began scratching through alleys for scrap wood. Depression was clawing into Canada in the 1870s and the working class was being crushed. Most didn't even have the right to vote for change. In Ontario, the law required men to pay local tax on at least $400 a year in order to vote. It was a huge burden for the working poor, whose average yearly wage was only $390. Voters making less than $800 didn't have to pay taxes—it was considered too low an income—but they lost the right to vote. Ontario also required some form of property ownership. Tom Phillips thought it was a national shame and wrote scathingly against the Income Franchise Bill in 1874: "The Dominion makes laws which affect the poorest as well as the wealthiest. It is perfectly absurd to take the question of payment of local assessments into consideration.... Contributing to local taxation has no legitimate bearing upon his position in respect to the Dominion Government." Ontario would cancel its property provision in 1884, but it would take over forty years for Parliament to enact a standard, dominion-wide franchise in 1920.

The Depression also claimed Tom Phillips. Two years after its launch, *The National* collapsed and he had to scrounge for work. In 1876 he became an emigrant again, moving his family across the invisible border to Boston. It would be three lean years before they returned to Canada. Delia worried about him in her diary: "Nov. 1, 1876, Mass.: What a fine afternoon it is, though dreary enough for us, but Tom will soon be home. I think how patiently he has given up so many things—how he gets up in the morning and walks to Town, coming home so promptly."

Tom Phillips walked to work at the *Boston Traveller* to save tram fare. There wasn't money for any domestic help, either; one of Delia's sisters, Edie, moved in to assist with the children. But it was a lively time for lively minds. Thompson and Delia burrowed into the bohemian intelligentsia, mixing with Emerson and Longfellow. Delia scribbled in her diary about the thrill of meeting fellow Canadian Graham Bell: "April 18, 1877: Professor Bell has been giving lectures explaining the telephone....Mr. Bell put his mouth to the instrument. Four miles off someone sang God Save the Queen. I wonder if we will ever fly to each other. At the rate of such things we will—if we do not get too fat."

Tom Phillips returned to Canada to a job on the editorial staff of the Toronto *Mail* in 1879, but his four-year-old son became suddenly sick. It would be years before Delia could even write about it:

"Our sweet little Tom. How well he was in the evening playing with his papa—wishing he was a *Mail* boy so that he could bring papa's papers in the morning and when he got to be a man he would make papers like Papa....I will never forget the croup that rang through the house. Papa went for the doctor....I saw a change—ah that change. His eyes seemed blinded like with a great light. 'Mama,' he said, 'put out the light' and 'Papa, I want Papa.'

"It was between 3 and 4 o'clock of that Wednesday morning, 25th of February when he went."

Stillness always follows the death of a child. Then the heart must decide to open or close. In 1880, Tom Phillips was at a crossroads. The *Globe* had offered to send him to Ireland to report on the Land League uprisings—the Irish poor were refusing to pay their rents to their landlords. Tom Phillips was sceptical of the Irish and of their rabble-rousing leader Charles Stewart Parnell. He'd already seen the Fenians' murderous skills along the Canadian border, but he went in spite of himself. For three months he tramped across the island, listening patiently to every point of view, observing conditions that no amount of talk could obscure. What he saw challenged his faith in the goodness of man and widened his heart forever.

> *The Globe*, January 10, 1882: The land is utterly inadequate for the population, rent or no rent. The difficulty is chronic and permanent. Multitudes are always struggling on the verge of destitution—wretchedly clad, poorly fed, overwhelmed with debt....And so, in spite of blunders and crimes, and defeats—in spite of the greed of the self-seeking and the ambitions of the demagogues—through bloodshed, and tears, and suffering, the cause of the People will prevail by slow degrees, and the accumulated and buttressed wrongs of centuries be overthrown.

His dispatches from Ireland moved his readers so deeply that the *Globe* reprinted them in an extra edition. "He told a plain story," the *Buffalo Courier* reported. "He allowed no word of rage to escape him, though it was clearly to be seen that underneath the man's calmness his blood was boiling." Ireland had made Tom Phillips a different calibre of reporter, capable of engaging the social conscience of a nation. He promised never to ridicule the poor again.

He was invited everywhere to talk and became one of the country's best platform speakers, which helped supplement his meagre income. But he needed an intellectual home, something truer than the backbiting scrabble of partisan journalism. His mind had turned to the cause of social justice, and Edmund Sheppard shared his fury.

Sheppard had left the conservative *Mail* and lured Tom Phillips away from the *Globe* to be the assistant editor and chief editorial writer of his bold new venture. The *Toronto News* began as a four-page daily selling for two cents. Its tag line was definitive: "Hostile to the Divine rights of kings and a titled or privileged class." On the first day of publication, it demanded the separation of church and state and the abolishment of the office of governor general. By the next year it was the largest evening daily in the city, edging out the *Telegram*. Here was where the reporter Tom Phillips became an activist, and where writing became an act of passion.

Toronto, the Queen City, had become a study in contrasts. While the 1880s had brought prosperity to the well-off, slums were appearing like cankers, rents for the poor doubled in ten years and children made up eleven percent of the city's workforce. Many lived on the streets. Newspapers blamed the poor, as they always did, insinuating a lack of Christian morals and work ethic. Tom Phillips watched the press chase the poor like criminals right through the century, all the way up to the crash of '29, when the unemployed held up their job qualifications on placards while the well-off threw them change and busted up their unions. He was sure he could change the world. In his column, Tom Phillips gave the poor a face and a soul.

> The night hawks of a great city like Toronto are...boys and girls and even children of tender years. They are deserving of some attention, which I intend they will

> receive. The poor, homeless, friendless outcasts make the street their home. They are the sport of chance & the children of misfortune. They find themselves fighting for existence years before the children of the well to do. The wonder is that any attain to good citizenship as not a few have done. In spite of their poverty they are not all bad.

Tom Phillips was becoming Canada's Charles Dickens, making the poor visible to a country that preferred to punish them. He had the "pen of a revolutionist and the heart of a gentle, loving woman," according to his *Toronto News* partner, Edmund Sheppard. Soft-spoken Tom Phillips became notorious for his politely argued positions, held as lethally as a pistol to the head. He was almost alone in his defence of the working class and in the pursuit of social equality. A great nation, he believed, should be a just one.

When the labour movement came marching into Canada in the 1880s, the *Toronto News* endorsed the Knights of Labour, becoming the *de facto* workingman's paper. Tom Phillips could see that this was a different kind of union.

The Noble and Holy Order of the Knights of Labour was an American union that had first crossed into Hamilton in 1875. It stressed moral character, education and brotherhood. Unlike other trade unions, it was breaking down class lines among workers themselves. Skilled and unskilled banded together, black, white, French and English. The order's code of principles included securing the right of workers to the full enjoyment of the wealth they created, enough time off to develop intellectual and moral faculties, the end of child labour for those under sixteen, and the protection of public land for settlers, not speculators. Tom Phillips spoke for them publicly and wrote passionately for their *Palladium of Labour*. Though not nearly as widely read as the *News*, it was far more radical.

In July of 1883, Tom Phillips and the News geared up for a major confrontation. The Knights of Labour were organizing a telegraph strike that promised to be decisive. Canada's first international strike for equal pay was waged against two powerful companies: Western Union and Great North Western. Workers walked out en masse, 1,200 Canadians and 18,000 Americans, holding firm for a while. But the companies were intransigent and when the strike was finally called off in August, Tom Phillips fumed.

> *Palladium of Labour*, September 23, 1883: The great strike of the telegraph operators is ended. It is a humiliating defeat....Where is that sublime and boasted figure "public sympathy" now...their mere sympathy amounts to practically nothing. An ounce of brains is worth more than a pound of sympathy....You defeated telegraph operator, who has been always so anxious to keep communistic ideas out of the meetings—I ask you, how under Heaven you ever expect to get a fair day's wages from Jay Gould [a prominent owner] so long as you refuse to discuss in your brotherhood the right to monopoly by which he can blacklist you. Are

> not his millions of telegraph poles planted in the people's land?...In so far as trade unions persist in boycotting ideas and refusing to take unto themselves brains they are no better than their oppressors....In the last analysis there can be no real victory for labour without ideas.

Tom Phillips would not bite his tongue, not for the unions and not for the capitalists. Silence he thought, was betrayal. Implacability made him few friends, but he was looking for justice.

In 1885 he suddenly quit the *Toronto News* over the North-West Rebellion, refusing to write editorials supporting the execution of Louis Riel. He didn't think the Métis leader was a traitor; back in 1971 when the Fenians were counting on his support, Riel had raised loyalist volunteers to defend the frontier. He had successfully argued for Métis rights in the formation of Manitoba in 1870 and had tried to do the same thing in Saskatchewan. Riel had seized the church at Batouche but when the North-West Mounted Police arrived, he'd had no choice but to fight back. History was recorded by the winners, Tom Phillips knew.

He also knew that English Canada was almost unanimous in demanding a public hanging, especially Ontario's Orange Lodge, which had never forgiven Riel for executing Protestant surveyor Thomas Scott back in Manitoba. But there was no point to killing Riel, Tom Phillips reasoned; Riel was a pitiful man by then, considered insane, having suffered a nervous breakdown, believing he was on a divine mission of God. Nonetheless, "the cowards in Ottawa, and their subordinates in Regina" committed him to trial. Outside French Canada, Phillips stood almost alone in defending the Métis leader.

> *Palladium of Labour*, July 11, 1885: Vindictive partisans of government are gleefully rubbing their corruption-smirched hands with delight at the prospect of a wholesale hanging. Not satisfied with the blood poured out at Batouche and Cut Knife Hill, and the spectacle of bereaved women and children deprived of means of subsistence and slowly perishing of starvation with none to help them, these infuriated loyalists clamour for more blood. Riel must hang!...The government organs are inspired by the desire to make political capital—to whitewash Sir John and his colleagues with the blood of the half breeds. The government has been justly blamed for provoking the outbreak by its long continued neglect of the just claims of the half breeds and the white settlers by its favouritism to land speculators and monopolists and by the robberies of its hordes of rascally agents and officials....If anybody is guilty of treason, if anyone deserves death for purely political offences, it is those who have caused this outbreak....Wouldn't you as a last resort have grabbed your rifle and fought against extermination? I hope so.

Defending Riel had been politically blasphemous, maybe even treasonous. Louis Riel was executed in Regina on November 16, and Tom Phillips was never hired again by any of the major newspapers. By 1888 he was almost penniless. Though physical poverty held no terror for him, intellectual poverty was abhorrent. Money was useful for the books it could buy you, not status.

Tom Phillips was forced to sell the family home and got a tidy sum. Instead of banking it or investing, he went on a learning holiday to England with his wife and three daughters. The girls would remember it as the most glorious time of their lives. When they returned, the Orange Order was still stirring up a froth against the French, dividing a new Canada. Tom Phillips had finally accepted the distinctiveness of French Canada as a necessary fact of nationhood:

"Corruption in politics is bad, but race and creed war is infinitely worse....Class supremacy in any form is a hateful thing, but if it must be—if the feelings between Catholic and Orangemen is so intense and deep-seated that no *modus vivendi* can be arrived at other than the ascendancy of one or the other—the Catholic, the Jesuit if you will, is on the whole preferable to the Orangeman. The Jesuit is at least a gentleman and a man of the world. The Orangeman is too often either a fanatic or a self-seeker affecting fanaticism to serve his personal ends."

Tom Phillips held to his allegiances and causes, writing for the smaller papers like the *Palladium*; battling, sometimes single-handedly, the capitalist forces that aimed to erase the face of working men and women. He was a member of the Single Tax Association, the Nationalist Club, the Anti-poverty Society, the Trades and Labour Congress, the Toronto Suffrage Association and the Toronto Conference on Social Problems. He championed so many lost causes that would later be found by history: the eight-hour work day, streetcars on Sunday, votes for women: "The eight hour day is gaining strength rapidly....Working women in particular cannot hope to gain shorter hours except by legislative enactment, and they suffer most of all."

And while critical of the short-sightedness of labour, Tom Phillips never gave up hope or help when it came to the unions. He worked to establish a Canadian Populist party of workers and farmers, he wrote a collection of his own union songs, he ran unsuccessfully as a Labour Reform candidate in a provincial election. He was never afraid of rejection.

In 1891 he founded his last newspaper, a radical weekly called the *Labor Advocate*. His opinions had matured; his long-held suspicion about the futility of labour strikes softened into a lament and a plea.

> *Labor Advocate*, February 27, 1891: Fighting great combinations of capital by the old-fashioned methods of the strike and the boycott in this age is a good deal like opposing a force armed with Armstrong guns and Winchester rifle, with flint lock muskets. The capitalists everywhere are organizing in opposition to labour unions....To confine organized effort to fighting employers for higher wages or shorter hours is to

> invite defeat. Organize for political action, should be the watchword. Working men must combine to use their ballots as a lever to oppose consolidated capitalism.

The federal government finally honoured Canadian workers by officially adopting Labour Day as a national holiday in 1894.

The years were disappearing and Tom Phillips had somehow raced through middle age, through twenty-five years of marriage, through fatherhood—his girls growing into young women so suddenly. And then Delia was gone, dying of a stroke in 1897. Her sister Edie had to go too—unmarried women were not allowed to live under the same roof as unmarried men, widowed or not. Tom Phillips had to send her off to work for another family out of town. Two years later he received an urgent telegram: Tom Phillips went at once to fetch and marry her. They had a son named Phillip and as a fifty-three-year-old father, he must have seemed like Methuselah. It was certainly against the norm to marry his dead wife's sister, but the laws of convention never much mattered to Tom Phillips, nor the observances of faith. He was emphatically secular. But faith was preferred over blind nationalism. In1905, Tom Phillips Thompson supported the creation of separate schools in the new prairie provinces: "If children must be taught to worship anything, it is better that they should adore the Virgin Mary of Rome than prostrate themselves before the great god Jingo or the flag that is the emblem of class and caste rule at home." He was a socialist to the end.

He lived out his last years in Oakville, scribbling missives to the editorial pages, freelancing for educational and industry magazines, and for the *Labour Gazette*, as the Toronto correspondent. Every year his birthday was duly marked by the visit of some cub reporter and by a little notice in the papers. In 1929, *The Mail* recorded: "Phillips Thompson, veteran newspaperman, celebrates his 86th birthday."

Tom Phillips went blind slowly, the light fading only on the outside, not the inside, as he kept writing at his desk. When sight failed completely, he dictated to his daughter, Maud. His mind continued to bristle at the capitalists and union busters, the self-serving politicians and ham-fisted editors who got in the way of social justice. He saw the past repeat itself in the agony of the Great Depression.

But the old bones were tired. Tom Phillips had done what he could to stop the privilege of class, taking the best of what was English to beat out what was worst.

Over the years he'd written faithfully to his two grandchildren in the Yukon, Pierre and Lucy Berton. The last letter was a poem, dictated on November 29, 1932.

Dear Pierre and Lucy,

I feel fine,
Now that my years are 89.
With presents and congratulations
From many friends and dear relations
Whose thoughtfulness and loving kindness

Cheers my old age and partial blindness....
And so with confidence and cheer
I enter on my 90th year.
I have no other news to tell
Except that we're all feeling well,
For things go on from day to day
In pretty much the same old way.
And so I pause to light my pipe
And get Aunt Maud these lines to type.
Your loving grandfather, Phillips Thompson.

Tom Phillips Thompson died of a stroke on May 20, 1933, while dictating to his daughter, Maud. It was left to his colleagues in the press, the rogues and gentlemen, to make of his life what they would. What they did was forget him, erasing him out of most of the history books, or making his name a small footnote to other people's legacies. His obituary in the *Toronto Star* on May 21, 1933, offered some of the last fine words written about him.

> The late Mr. Phillips Thompson was in his day a clear-sighted and just-minded journalist. He was one of the gentlest of men, but utterly incapable of pretending to agree in a matter of opinion with you or with the King of England if he did not so agree. There was a mild but firm force in him. One wonders how many of the newspapermen of today owe something to the example of this always soft-spoken and sincere man who, at the age of ninety, goes forth to his burial in

Oakville. He spoke for the inarticulate, he was on the side of lost causes, he could show you that minorities, although out-numbered, were usually right.

English Immigration History in Canada

Despite public perception and the murky myths of history, not all English immigrants were wealthy or privileged. In the nineteenth century, the English who came to Canada were often pulled by economic reasons. In Dickensian England, many working people were unemployed and struggling just to eat. T. Phillips Thompson had watched his own father go bankrupt twice. Thompson was fourteen when he left England's industrial north to start over in Ontario. One of the attractions was the colony's decidedly English cultural roots.

The English had been laying claim to Canada since 1497, when King Henry VII sent John Cabot sailing across the sea in the *Matthew*. Calling what was probably Prince Edward Island St. John's Island, Cabot planted the flag of England, unfurling the first European colours in the New World. Fifty years later, John Rut made it to St. John's Newfoundland, under the patronage of Henry VIII and sent the first recorded letter from North America. Then the crowds moved in—Martin Frobisher looking for a Northwest Passage while kidnapping Inuit (1576), Humphrey Gilbert trying to start a colony (1583), followed by John Davis (1585), George Waymouth (1602), Henry Hudson (1609) and William Baffin (1615). In 1621 King James I granted Acadia to his Scottish poet friend, William Alexander, who'd argued that the Scots needed a New Scotland just as much as a New France or a New England. Alexander became Lord Protector of Nova Scotia and the English had a colony.

Serious migration began in the Atlantic colonies with the foundation of Halifax in 1749. Two-thirds of its early population of 3,000 was English, planted there as a counter force to the French at Louisbourg. When Louisbourg was captured in 1758 and Quebec in 1759, and with the Treaty of Paris in 1763, New France became another British colony. In the 1760s, New England farmers of English descent settled around the Bay of Fundy on former Acadian lands. In the early 1770s, a group of Yorkshiremen put down roots in northern Nova Scotia.

At the end of the American War of Independence, a flood of Loyalists scurried northward. While politically motivated, these immigrants from colonies in the United States received special status and land grants in return for their loyalty to the British Crown. The majority settled in what became the province of New Brunswick, while some English-Americans immigrated to what became Upper Canada in 1791. Later still, a small number of Loyalists went to the prairies for farming opportunities, attracted by offers of free land.

By 1819, half of the British subjects who sailed for British North America were English from the British Isles. Many of these immigrants were officially encouraged or given some means of assistance. England was the imperial centre, the "Old Country" by definition, and up until 1867, many of the English came in official capacities as public servants and soldiers. When they were released from service, many stayed on. Almost all the officials in British Columbia when the province entered Confederation in 1871, were English or Anglo-Irish.

By 1851 the first wave of English immigration had waned. Four more substantial waves of English immigration were still to come. Following Confederation, orphans came from private homes as well as industrial schools and poor-law schools. Granted free passage, thousands of British children, most of them English, were settled across Canada as wards of various societies between 1867 and the 1920s.

Another influx of English settlers, lured by the opening of the Prairie provinces, arrived in Canada between 1890 and 1914. In 1901 they numbered less than 10,000, but in 1906, three years after an immigration office was set up in central London, 65,000 immigrants arrived in Canada. In 1913 the number peaked at 113,004. The British government, under the Empire Settlement Act of 1922, helped 130,000 British immigrants settle in Canada after WW I. After World War II, in 1947, over 7,000 English, many of them trained industrial workers, artisans and technicians, immigrated to Canada. In 1957 the number rose to 75,546; in 1967 the number dropped to 43,000.

Overcoming Obstacles

In settling the colonies in British North America, the imperial authorities wanted to reproduce the English class system. Hoping to establish an aristocracy, ex-officers and members of the gentry were encouraged to settle with generous offers of land. But the colony was chafing under imperialism.

By the 1860s, Toronto was humming with talk of Confederation and Englishman T. Phillips Thompson entered the debate about whether Canada should inherit all things British or become a republic. He published his opinion in 1864. In a small booklet he called *"The Future*

Government of Canada," Thompson served up some harsh words for the country that had ruined his father:

> The time must come for Canada to cease her present connection with the British Empire. Canada can exist as an independent nation, not a monarchy or aristocracy. What could be more ridiculous than to bestow class privileges because of the achievements of some remote ancestor? Remove class distinction and bestow upon all the same advantages, regardless of race, creed, colour or condition. Give all a fair start in the race of life.

The opposite occurred. Speculative companies such as the Canada Company acquired large tracts of land on the condition that they bring "suitable" settlers from England. Schemes were introduced by which English parishes unloaded paupers and victims of crop failures and economic depression into Canada. They came with no means of survival and no skills necessary to endure the pioneer experience.

Wherever the English settled, they quickly assimilated into the local community. They didn't have to learn a new language and there was little prejudice against them, except for the early English immigrants who'd populated Quebec and the occasional protests lobbed their way—in the early 1900s, "Englishmen Need Not Apply" signs were posted throughout the prairies. Resentment of English immigrants peaked in times of economic strain. During the depression of the early 1900s, the government dealt as severely with English immigrants as with others. In 1908, 1,800 people were deported, 1,100 of whom were returned to the British Isles.

The English were very widely and evenly spread across Canada and considered themselves the founding people of the country. As a result, they tended to be less self-defensively clannish than other immigrant populations. The occasional all-English agrarian settlements usually existed because their members shared the same class attitudes or the same opinions rather than because of an imposed segregation or lack of acceptance by the wider society.

The English-Canadian Legacy

A number of Canadian institutions have been inherited or influenced by English models. The parliamentary system of government, under which the cabinet rules the country and is responsible to Parliament, is an extension of the British cabinet system. It was set up in the colonial government as outlined in the British North America Act of 1867. In the realm of law, the civil law in Canadian provinces (with the exception of Quebec, where the French civil code is maintained) is based largely on English common law. And the justice system of Canadian courts also closely follows the English example.

The Anglican Church, formerly the Church of England in Canada, is one of the most predominant and distinctively English institutions in the country. It was transplanted almost unchanged from the homeland. About half all Canadians of English descent adhere to the

Anglican faith. The remainder belong to the United Church, as well as to a few smaller Protestant sects. Community-enhancing institutions such as the Red Cross, the Boy Scouts and the Girl Guides were also brought from England.

Canada's political parties have also been deeply influenced by England. In particular, the New Democratic Party (previously the Co-operative Commonwealth Federation) follows the tradition of democratic socialism represented by the British Independent Labour Party (later the Labour Party). The party was founded and built in Canada by English, Welsh and Scots and has always operated more like an Anglo-Scottish party than an American one; its structure of constituency branches combined with its ties to labour unions also reflect the Labour Party in Britain.

Along with their traditions of social democracy, English workers brought their own fierce traditions of labour unions. As a result, trade unionists from Britain made up the labour elite in Canada. T. Phillips Thompson is but one example. His father's failure had made young Thompson forever suspicious of capitalism and of class privilege. Thompson wrote in defence of the working class and the downtrodden. He promoted radical challenges to the emerging industrial capitalist society and became a spokesman for the Canadian branch of the Knights of Labour, the major labour reform organization of the late nineteenth century. Thompson was the author of the Knights' *Labour Reform Songster*, was a regular speaker at public events and wrote a column in the

Knight's newspaper, *The Palladium of Labour*. In 1887, he produced what has been described as the labour movement's most articulate critique, *The Politics of Labour*.

Sources

The Canadian Men and Women of the Time: A Handbook of Canadian Biography, Henry James Morgan, editor. W. Biggs, Toronto, 1898.

The Canadians, George Woodcock. Fitzhenry & Whiteside, Don Mills, 1979.

An English Sense of Justice, directed by Lindalee Tracey. White Pine Pictures, Toronto, 1999.

Essays in Canadian Working Class History, Gregory S. Kealey and Peter Warrian, editors. McClelland & Stewart, Toronto, 1976.

The Fitzhenry & Whiteside Book of Canadian Facts & Dates, Jay Myers. Fitzhenry & Whiteside, Richmond Hill, 1991.

I Married the Klondyke, Laura Beatrice Berton. McClelland & Stewart, Toronto, 1961.

Personal diaries of Delia Fisher Thompson, furnished by the Berton/Woodward families.

The Politics of Labor, Thomas Phillips Thompson. Belford, Clarke & Co, 1887.

The Regenerators: Social Criticism in Late Victorian English Canada, Ramsay Cook. University of Toronto Press, Toronto, 1984.

The Royal Commission on the Relations of Labour and Capital Report, 1889.

A Source Book of Canadian History: Selected Documents and Personal Papers, Harry S Crowe, Kenneth McNaught and J.H. Stewart Read. Longmans, Toronto, 1959.

Starting Out: 1920–1947, Pierre Berton. McClelland & Stewart, Toronto, 1987.

Sigursteinn and Stephanie Oddson

Chapter Five
Saga of Hope: Sigursteinn Oddson

Canada and the World in 1883

The Parliament Buildings at Quebec City are destroyed by fire.

The first session of the Northwest Territories Legislative Council is held in Regina.

The first issue of the *Calgary Herald* is published.

Standard Time is adopted by Canada.

The rotary snowplow is designed by CPR engineers.

The Toronto Women's Suffrage Association is founded.

Inoculation against anthrax is discovered.

The first skyscraper is built in Chicago.

Karl Marx, the German philosopher who co-wrote the *Communist Manifesto*, dies.

Augusta Stowe Gullen is the first woman doctor to graduate from a Canadian university.

Cardboard cartons, packaged flower seeds, rubber garden hoses, harmonicas, milk chocolate, ready-mixed paints, fountain pens, upright pianos, Hires root beer, toilet paper and typewriters are widely available in the 1880s.

Sigursteinn Oddson was raised in the Icelandic land of memory, on the sagas and poems that reached back a millennium, and had carried that memory across the sea. Now his own land is mute; only the trees speak, growing back like a hydra's head, like a curse on the dead.

Sigursteinn had cleared these Manitoba acres once, yet even his grave is uncertain in the great gobbling up of history. His name is a scrawl on a doctor's report and a ship's manifest, a neatly typed line on a land claim that almost doomed him. A century of amnesia has grown around Sigursteinn Oddson—strange for a people who remember everything. But who remembers the casualties of dreams?

Sigursteinn was born in 1863 on the desolate rump of an aching island. He was long and pale, with a held-in chin that made him seem cautious, or maybe dubious. It was a sad face, haunted like a poet's. Sigursteinn grew up in the wail of wind and worry, wanting to get free of the bad luck of Iceland. The force of nature had grown ferocious. In a century of hard winters, 1874 was almost the worst—snow and polar ice jammed up the ports and sheep had to be killed for lack of fodder. Then came the year of the falling ash when Mount Askja erupted, spewing hot lava on a big chunk of Iceland. There was nothing left to bury, no more forests, no more hope. There wasn't even wood for homes—Sigursteinn's family lived in a sod house, heated by the breath of livestock. There was no use complaining; the whole country was on its knees to Denmark.

Like all of Iceland, Sigursteinn clung to books and poetry, and to the Icelandic sagas—some of the most exquisite and fantastical works in all of Europe, heroic tales and sad ones, written with a precise knowledge of human tragedy. Icelanders remembered being mighty once—the most famed storytellers of Europe, the most literate. They had created the world's oldest parliament in A.D. 930;

they had ventured to the edges of the world. It was an Icelandic sea captain, Leif Eriksson, who had first laid claim to the New World he called Vinland, in A.D. 995. Now his descendants were barely citizens in their own country. They turned westward again, imagining.

A desperate Icelandic exploratory party went into Manitoba in 1875. The Canadian west needed immigrants; Manitoba was only five years old, a postage-stamp province that was giving away 160-acre homesteads. Icelanders needed a home. But the Red River was ravaged by grasshoppers and the open prairie scared them off. They nosed beyond the province, into the unsurveyed shore of Lake Winnipeg. It was magnificent—fish, meadows and poplar forests, a living place so starkly different from the crags and fjords of home. They raced back to Winnipeg and negotiated an Icelandic reserve with the Canadian government. Nyja Island—New Iceland—would be a district of Keewatin in the Northwest Territories, a self-governing territory under Ottawa's jurisdiction. A republic for a conquered people.

Its beginning was harrowing. The Icelanders set out at the start of autumn, not knowing that Lake Winnipeg would beat them back with ice and wind. They were forced ashore south of Gimli. There wasn't enough time to finish building before winter, or to collect enough fresh food, and the Icelanders crowded into half-made log houses. Scurvy killed almost all the young and old. In the spring, 1,200 new settlers arrived and by the fall a smallpox epidemic had killed over 100 more. The curse of history followed them into the New World.

Lord Dufferin, governor general of Canada, came to bolster the Icelanders with a speech on September 14, 1877:

> The three arts most necessary to the Canadian colonist are the felling of timber, the ploughing of land, and the construction of highways, but, as in your own country none of you had ever seen a tree, a cornfield or a road, it is not to be expected that you should immediately exhibit any expertness in these accomplishments, but practice and experience will soon make you master of all three.

For three years the Icelanders hammered together their settlement, bracing against floods, mosquitoes and religious feuding. A few left for North Dakota. And then a few more. By 1881, a handful of settlers remained. The republic needed people.

Only good news got back to Iceland, and hope. The Allan Line of Montreal began a busy passenger trade bringing Icelanders to Quebec City. Emigrants packed their Lutheran Bibles and books and crammed into steerage. In 1883 Sigursteinn Oddson got on board and took a last long look at the ragged edges of home. Whatever lay ahead had to be better.

The voyage took four weeks and the North Atlantic heaved. Then Sigursteinn travelled twelve days inland to Winnipeg on the transcontinental railway that had just been completed the year before. He settled among the Icelanders, in the area around the Eyjolfsson boarding house. His eyes wandered to the owner's pretty sister, Stefania. It was exhilarating, not just loving her and wanting to marry, but the fact that he could. Back in Iceland a landless man was not allowed to take a bride. Sigursteinn's ambition swelled up—he wanted land, something certain to put his name on. Something permanent. He went to the Dominion Land Office and picked out a section from a blurry map: Township 20, lot SE 16-20-5, in Lundar. The agents stumbled on his name and changed it to Samuel Oddson. Then Sigursteinn spent a few of his last dollars buying a marriage licence.

Sigursteinn and Stefania went by wagon to Cold Springs, to their land near Lake Manitoba. It was a low-lying section of meadow, grass and densely tangled poplars. Sigursteinn had rarely seen trees in Iceland, had rarely even heard their rustling. They were magical and strange, obscuring a sky that used to hang so wide in Iceland. Sometimes the trees seemed to stare down at him, watching, or to whisper conspiratorially above his head. Perhaps it was only his imagination.

It was an irony for a treeless people to have to cut down poplars, a kind of deep-down sacrilege that could turn an anxious mind fearful and suspicious. Sigursteinn was supposed to clear forty acres of land in three years to open it up for grain farming. All he had was a small axe and a pick to yank the roots up with. He began to hack.

First he built a log cabin for Stefania, an unimaginable luxury, and then a stable and a few sheds for his cows, chickens and sheep. Then he moved into the bush. These were long, hard days—muscle against trunk and tree root, buckets of sweat on the ground, the steeling of nerves as mosquitoes hummed and bit their way into his skin, the slow trickle of madness thickening the mind. Sigursteinn started to look like the trees he was cutting, his body twisting to their shape, his forearms bulging like knots.

The forest was moody. Sometimes he liked its hush and privacy, how it held him in by the force of damp gravity. He felt absorbed. Sometimes it was a separate thing, hostile in its secrets. Sigursteinn would often recite Icelandic verses, perhaps to prove his own existence or courage. At day's end, he stumbled toward the yellow light of his log cabin, feeling the certainty of ownership. Stephania would feed him boiled lamb and the skimmed milk yogurt the Icelanders called *skir*. There weren't many vegetables.

Icelanders weren't natural gardeners, and the Manitoba land was reluctant. Underneath the tree trunks the soil was thin and the subsoil clayey. It took coaxing to bring up potatoes and carrots or even turnips. The Icelandic settlers turned to their ancient skills with sheep and cattle. They also learned to ice fish—there wasn't time in the summer to get to the lake. Land clearing was an obligation—without cut-down trees, Sigursteinn risked forfeiting his claim.

Cash was scarce. Stefania worked on her woolens at night, carding, spinning, then knitting the wool for trade. Sigursteinn hired himself out as a manual labourer, digging ditches, harvesting other people's fields, working casual labour and railway jobs in Winnipeg. Mostly it was hand to mouth and almost everything came from the land. Always the trees took priority, taunting Sigursteinn with their stubbornness. He delighted in the small bald patches he could gouge in the ground, contemplating his pile of trees like a soldier counting the enemy's dead.

In 1886 Gudrun came, their first Canadian baby, named for the suffering heroine of ancient Icelandic poetry. Perhaps marked by it. Icelandic baby names were cropping up all over the reserve: Kristjans, Sigruns, Helgis, Olgas. New Iceland was growing up around Sigursteinn, spreading out from Gimli. The immigrants were setting up their own schools, clubs and systems, becoming what they couldn't be in Iceland. Settlers argued frantically in the editorial pages of their two newspapers, created book clubs and clustered around the general stores and Lutheran church. There was only the sound of Icelandic those first years until they gave up their self-governing rights. In 1887 New Iceland was incorporated into Manitoba and became the municipality of Gimli. When English teachers finally arrived and then the waves of Ukrainian immigrants, they called the Icelanders "Ghoulies."

Out in the bush the trees seemed to be growing back overnight. Sigursteinn couldn't cut them down and pick their roots out fast enough. He learned that another immigrant family had already tried to clear this land and failed. It was no place for sheep, either; they were getting twisted in the bush, and the coyotes and foxes were having their fill. There was nothing to do but keep hacking. Then his land flooded and all his efforts sank. It had been easy to choose land on a flood plain; those damn maps in

Winnipeg only showed numbered blocks of land. Nobody ever got to see the land before he picked a number. All over New Iceland sections were flooding and Icelanders were moving on to North Dakota. But Sigursteinn wouldn't budge. Maybe it was stubbornness, or pride. Maybe a man could only have one dream and had to see it to the end. Sigursteinn would not give up. His only hope was a new piece of land.

Sigursteinn was losing to the trees and the swamps. By 1891 he had become a naturalized citizen, for the good it did, and his second daughter, Katrin, was born. Other daughters followed: Olina in 1895 and Wilhelmina in 1900. There was no more money for a fourth child. Wilhelmina was sent to live with an aunt, fostered out.

It was a father's shame not to be able to provide for his child, another bruise in the wound of self. Sigursteinn could almost feel the trees laughing at him—those damned poplars with their yellow leaves flapping like hands over their grins. He was sure he could hear them whispering about his failure, about his stupidity, about how to make things worse. Even late at night when Stefania and the girls milked the cows, Sigursteinn could feel the trees way back in the dark, watching over him. The trees weren't retreating with his hacking, they were getting closer, growing into his dreams at night. It was a fight for survival and the trees were winning. He had his eye on a quarter section a few miles away and applied for it.

Sigursteinn was literate, a voracious reader of Icelandic poetry, and literature and the Bible. But English didn't fit so easily on his tongue and reading it was difficult, especially the rejection letters from the Dominion Land Office. Sigursteinn's anglicized name got stuck in the wheels of bureaucracy. For a long time the civil servants thought Samuel and Sigursteinn were two different people competing for the same parcel of land. Their legalese was daunting and Sigursteinn wrote again and again, over several years, always signing "Your obedient servant."

Sometimes Sigursteinn took a few drinks during those long days in the bush. Or hid a jar of brew in the shed. He'd been soothing himself quietly for years on the poisonous hooch that was boiled in the woods, the potato ethyl or turnip, corn—it didn't matter. Anything to take away the smallness, to get sugar in his mind and veins so he could feel swelled up and mighty. He wasn't alone. A temperance movement was started to control the access to alcohol in the area. There was so much more of it than there'd been in Iceland. The settlers weren't used to booze and some men were drowning in it.

Behind the booze was hurt and rage. All Sigursteinn ever wanted to do was farm. But he was losing control, sniping at the other settlers, lashing out physically.

A neighbour, a Mr. Halldorson, complained: "Sigursteinn Oddson was at my place last night and acted like a crazy man. He was using threats to people that were not there and I had to have men stay up with him all night. I believe the man to be insane and wish him to be arrested and taken to goal as I believe him to be dangerous to be at large."

There was just one place for people who didn't fit in. In 1901 Sigursteinn Oddson was committed to the Asylum for the Insane at Selkirk. According to admittance records he heard voices, couldn't sleep and was drunk all the time. More than likely he was suffering from acute alcohol poisoning and depression.

Stefania begged the Dominion Land Office to hold the section he had been so desperately requesting. She begged the asylum to let her husband out so he could clear his land. For three years Sigursteinn went in and out of Selkirk, drying out and cleaning up, only to return to the dark hissing of the trees. Was it really madness to feel persecuted when all of nature conspired against you, was it insane to prefer blankness to failure? In 1904 Sigursteinn got out of the asylum and made it home for good. A letter was waiting for him from the land office, approving his application for the new homestead. Section SW14-20-5 was finally his. Now new land would have to broken.

Already the first generation of New Icelanders was growing up and moving on, some to Winnipeg, some beyond. By 1906 the railway reached Gimli and passengers transformed the place from a pioneer settlement into a tourist and summer resort. Gudrun married a railway man and moved down the road, growing wordless in her husband's long absences. Grandchildren started appearing, taking their turns on Sigursteinn's knees—sore knees, bent in the shape of trees. Sigursteinn was still clearing land, planting hay now, seeing some financial return. The trees spoke less ferociously, their whispers no longer as malevolent. He built up his small place, getting eighteen head of cattle and some pigs. Putting up an acre of fencing and digging a nineteen-foot well. These were the good years, sandwiched between bad. The tender years as remembered in a poem by his grandson Hermann Sveinson:

In Lundar pioneer time, the Oddsons came from Iceland's far off shore
Lundar was also the town our parents chose and welcome marked their door
I remember happy visits to granpa's home, just down the road in sight
We children blissful unaware as tragic trouble darkened the happy light.

Luck is finite. In the living of dreams, sometimes the dreamer is sacrificed, eaten whole, gone mad or bad on land too big, too wet, too hard. Killed slowly by disappointment. In the heaving up a new nation, there were always the few who fell under trains, in debt, in the sinkhole of loneliness—their lives a caution to others; their deaths an appeasement to the fates. Sometimes their bad luck extended generations.

Sigursteinn's daughter Gudrun walked into a swamp and tried to die. She was sent to the same asylum in Selkirk where her father had been incarcerated, and slowly vanished. So did her eight children, one and two at a time, fostered across Canada, beaten and terrorized by their custodians. A whole branch of the family, severed.

In 1918, Stefania died—some think of stomach disease, others say she fell down a well. Her last glimpse of hope might have been a dark, wet hole. It was a sudden ending. Sigursteinn began to fade away, growing tired and sick. He was no longer tormented by the trees, but soothed by their shade in that last hot summer. He died in 1920 in Lundar, nursed by a neighbour and by his long-lost daughter Wilhelmina.

Too soon he was called to his rest, we all missed him so
No more his kindly eyes and magic voice and kindness know
He too had missed so much our dear grandma who had gone two years before.
Some say just to prepare their heavenly home and to greet him at its door.

There is little that remains of one man's efforts: a family Bible passed through the generations, and the land he cleared. It was sixty acres by the end, with ground too thin to plant much on. Only poplar roots could stand up in its clay. And one Icelandic man, teetering against the fates. Trying so hard not to give up.

In a land of hope, the unlucky leave their own mark. Upon their disappointments a name survives, and an attachment to the dignity of hard work.

Icelandic Immigration History in Canada

Sigursteinn Oddson was just a child when a devastating volcano erupted in his native Iceland. The ruin that followed forced an exodus of Icelanders to search for a new homeland. Iceland had a history of calamity and natural disasters. By 1800, the population had been reduced to 47,000 from 50,000 a century before by the scouring of disease, starvation and volcanic eruptions. The nineteenth century heaped on more bad luck with an epidemic that destroyed the sheep, climate deterioration and other volcanic eruptions. The entire population was offered resettlement in Denmark, but the Icelanders declined, knowing that the tyrannical rule of Denmark wouldn't allow them rights and freedoms as an independent people. Rumours started circulating about the natural wealth and milder climate of North America, and the possibility of their own self-governing settlement. Vinland was an ancient place, braided into Icelandic mythology. It was the Icelander Eric the Red who'd discovered the continent in A.D. 995.

Sigtryggur Jonasson was the first Icelandic immigrant to Canada since his Norse ancestors had sailed away. He arrived in Quebec City in 1872. Jonasson wrote optimistic letters back home about the area he'd settled in Ontario. About 150 Icelanders followed in 1873. Canadian immigration authorities at Quebec offered the group free transportation to Ontario, temporary quarters and 200 acres of free land per household. The Icelanders made their way to Rosseau in the Muskoka district but soon found that the promised government jobs, which were supposed to keep them employed until their land was cleared, were a little skimpy. Most of the settlers soon dispersed, leaving behind only a small permanent settlement.

A second group of over 300 Icelanders arrived in 1874. Sigtryggur Jonasson, then an agent for the Ontario government, took the group to Kinmount, northwest of Toronto, where work on the Victoria railroad was waiting for them. But when the work ran out, prospects for a sustainable Icelandic settlement faded.

Sigtryggur Jonasson contacted the minister of immigration in Ottawa about finding a suitable site for Icelandic settlers. An expedition was financed to explore the Red River Valley. But the region was ravaged by grasshoppers and the expedition continued north to the unsurveyed shore of Lake Winnipeg, beyond Manitoba's boundary. The Icelanders liked the area: it was located on water, had an abundance of fishing and timber, as well as a good location along potential transportation routes. When the delegation returned to Kinmount, the settlers quickly voted to move west. They were so anxious to leave that they abandoned crops and sold cows at half price. In 1875 about 235 Icelanders made the trek west by steamship, railway and then again by water on flatboats.

Home was an Icelandic reserve in what was then an uncharted part of the Northwest Territories—fifty miles along Lake Winnipeg's west shore. The reserve, established by an order-in-council and named New Iceland, was a unique political structure in Canadian history. Settlers could create their own laws, set up their own schools and generally operate with autonomy. The name Gimli, referring to a "gold thatched hall" of the Norse gods, was decided on for the capital of the new settlement.

By this time, Jonasson had returned to Iceland to stir up interest in New Iceland. In 1876, 1,200 more Icelanders, commonly known as the Large Group, joined the first inhabitants of New Iceland, creating the basis for the first permanent Icelandic settlement in Canada.

Icelanders continued to immigrate to Winnipeg through the end of the nineteenth century and into the next. Between the 1870s and 1914, one-fifth of the population of Iceland left their island home, many for Canada, including Sigursteinn Oddson, who arrived in 1883. The main centre of New Iceland, as anticipated, was Gimli, and the entire settlement eventually became a part of the province of Manitoba. Rural areas of Manitoba were also settled by Icelanders, including Lundar, Glenboro, Selkirk and Morden.

Overcoming Obstacles

Sigursteinn Oddson, like so many Icelanders, set out for Canada with high hopes of owning his own land and of escaping the curse of Icelandic calamity.

Natural disasters dated as far back as the Black Death of 1402 to 1404, which killed two-thirds of the population. Danish trade restrictions and the scourge of a stalled economy crippled Iceland's development during the 1860s. The winter of 1874 was the severest of the century. And 1875, although mild, brought earthquakes and more volcanic activity, climaxing in the tremendous eruption of Mount Askja, which blew smoke and clumps of glowing volcanic ash over nearby communities.

Nor had the immigrants in New Iceland escaped hardship. In the settlement's first winter of 1875, several settlers died of scurvy and starvation. The Large Group of immigrants who'd arrived from Iceland the following summer were lucky because the land had already been broken and sufficient equipment and supply routes established. But there were terrible surprises. In the fall of 1876, an unfamiliar disease appeared among the settlers. Mild at first, it quickly spread throughout the entire colony. Sigtryggur Jonasson, who was now living in Lundar and known as the Father of New Iceland, sent for a physician and medical supplies from Manitoba.

Poor housing made it inevitable that the disease would reach epidemic proportions in the colony. The weather had turned cold and many of the settlers hadn't finished construction on their dwellings. As a result, several families crowded into a single building, sharing clothes and blankets contaminated with the disease. By December a doctor had arrived and reported that the illness was smallpox. A vaccine sent up from the United States proved useless. Among the settlers, about one in three caught the disease. It killed 102, mostly children and young adults.

A quarantine was set up to prevent the epidemic from reaching the province of Manitoba. No one could leave the colony without waiting two weeks at the quarantine line. Work stood still and the economy of New Iceland faltered. Settlers were so discouraged they were making plans to leave the colony for good.

An exodus to Winnipeg and North Dakota began in 1878. There were just too many disappointments to bear.

The Icelanders had cleared the land, but no markets were found for their timber. Floods ravaged the farms, destroying gardens and fields and sweeping away houses and haystacks. Money was scarce and many had to seek temporary work outside of the colony. Roads were poor, unsafe or nonexistent. The smallpox epidemic was followed by scarlet fever a few months later, and then diphtheria and measles. By 1881, the population of New Iceland had shrunk to 250.

New immigrants continued to come to New Iceland, and by 1900 the population had bounced back to 2,000. But Sigursteinn Oddson had fractured on the hardships of starting over, one more casualty in a decade of broken dreams. His land proved swampy and his crops reluctant. Hard work wasn't always enough.

The Icelandic-Canadian Legacy

Literacy is the lifeblood of the Icelanders. The nation of Iceland has the highest literacy rate in the world, with more books, periodicals and newspapers published per capita than anywhere else on the planet. Sigursteinn Oddson was a typical Icelander and brought his Icelandic love of literature—poetry, books and his Lutheran Bible—with him to Canada.

One of the most unifying and enduring themes in Icelandic culture is the literature celebrating the sagas and settlement of Iceland. In Iceland's dark ages, the sagas and the skaldic poetry and ballads were a source of inspiration. The sagas are known for their terse, swift narrative, dramatic quality, detailed characterization and vivid portrayal of individual and community life. They emphasize courage, loyalty, friendship and close-knit family ties.

The Icelanders in Canada nurtured the literary tradition of their homeland. For years they've kept up the practice of reading aloud in the evenings, with the subject matter frequently becoming the topics of later conversation.

They have produced many poets and novelists writing in both English and Icelandic. Stephan G. Stephansson is considered by many critics to be the foremost Icelandic poet of this century. Guttormur J. Guttormsson was born in New Iceland in 1878 and did not visit Iceland until 1939. He was best known for the poem "Sandy Bar," a tribute to the Icelandic pioneers. Contemporary Icelandic writers include the late Laura Goodman Salverson, winner of the Governor General's Award, author of *The Viking Heart* (portraying the hardships endured by the Icelandic pioneers, their aspirations and achievements) and *Confessions of an Immigrant's Daughter*. She was also the first editor of the *Icelandic Canadian Magazine*.

It was the Icelandic National League of North America, perhaps the most important association in the history of Icelandic immigrants, that started the *Icelandic Canadian Magazine*, the first English-language Icelandic publication on the continent. The league was founded in 1919 to assist Icelanders to adapt to Canada and to preserve Icelandic heritage. Chapters sprang up in almost every settlement and in the cities where numbers of Icelanders relocated.

In 1951 a chair in Icelandic language and literature was established at the University of Manitoba. The Icelandic Collection in the University of Manitoba library has a full-time curator and over 14,000 volumes. It was there, in its stacks, that stories like those of Sigursteinn Oddson are to be found—a place where distant Icelandic descendants can become reacquainted with their heritage and retrace their roots.

Sources

Emigration from Iceland to North America, Don Gislason. *The Scandinavian Forum,* Winter 1987.

The Fitzhenry & Whiteside Book of Canadian Facts & Dates, Jay Myers. Fitzhenry & Whiteside, Richmond Hill, 1991.

Gimli Saga, Paul H.T. Thorlakson, editor. D.W. Friesen and Sons Ltd, Altona, 1975.

A History of Manitoba, Volume Two: Gateway to the West. Great Plains Publications, Winnipeg, 1994.

The Icelandic People in Manitoba: a Manitoba Saga, Wilhelm Kristjanson. Wallingford Press, Winnipeg, 1965.

Manitoba 125, A History, Volume II. Great Plains Publications, Winnipeg, 1994.

A Manitoba Saga, The Icelandic People in Manitoba, Wilhelm Kristjanson. Kristjanson, Winnipeg, 1965.

Wagons to Wings, History of Lundar and Districts, compiled by the Lundar and District Historical Society, Lundar, Manitoba.

Lem Wong

Chapter Six
The Road Chosen: Lem Wong

Canada and the World in 1897

The Victorian Order of Nurses is founded in Ottawa.

Gold is discovered at Lake Wawa, Ontario.

Prime Minister Wilfrid Laurier sails to England to attend Queen Victoria's Diamond Jubilee.

St. Francis Xavier College in Nova Scotia is the first Catholic college in North American to grant degrees to women graduates.

William McKinley is inaugurated as U.S. president.

Turkey declares war on Greece.

Gas-heated bathtubs, bicycles, packaged breakfast food, home cleansers and fishing reels become available in the 1890s.

Lem Wong arrived on a great gust of courage, a boy of fourteen sent on the hope and whispers of his mother. He had promised to work hard as a *gum sahn hak,* a guest of the Golden Mountain. But Lem had come at the boot end of the welcome. British Columbia was closing its door to the Chinese.

Lem hung close to his uncle that first day, oblivious to the sour stares of white Vancouver. He mimicked the old man as he bowed his shaved head and pigtail to the immigration men and paid his $50 head tax. Lem's occupation was officially recorded as "woodcutter." It was hardly believable for such a small boy. He would only reach five-foot-one when his growing was done.

Lem was already a man in China, the eldest son of a suddenly widowed mother, with a brother and sister to feed. Lem had heard the rumours snaking around Canton about the Golden Mountain and the heaps of money to be made there. For fifty years Chinese had been crossing the sea, building the Central Pacific railroad in Nevada, then moving north to the Cariboo goldfields and the Canadian Pacific Railway, arriving even before British Columbia had become a part of Canada in 1871. Seventeen thousand Chinese had blasted through the Rockies and laid down steel rails through British Columbia. Sometimes they had returned to China, looking for brides.

Lem didn't know the Chinese had only been paid half the wages of white men, or that 1,500 had died along the track. When the job ended in 1885, Chinese went scratching for work in the salmon canneries and in the mines as scab labour. Every year after, the hate had grown thicker against them, and the jobs had got thinner. Still, it was better than starving in China, the old Chinese would say.

Lem and his uncle followed the singsong of Cantonese into Chinatown, looking for work along the rickety storefronts on Carroll and Dupont streets. There were crowds of Chinese merchants in their quilted tunics and red-buttoned caps; coolies in shabby overalls, and "washee men" balancing their laundry bundles on poles across their backs. Here were the Chinese clans pooling their money into businesses and the Benevolent Societies. Here were the furtive pleasures: the gambling and opium, and the indentured prostitutes servicing the single men. The Presbyterians and Methodists had set up missions, too, with beds and English lessons. Lem took a job in a Chinese laundry and attended church classes. He trained his mouth to open wide around the English words. And he began to decipher the taunts that followed the Chinese like a bad smell. "Ching Chong Chinaman, chop, chop tail."

It surprised Lem that his pigtail was offensive. Under the Ch'ing Dynasty it was mandatory, a sign of oppression imposed by the northern Manchus who had conquered China four hundred years before. The queue was a symbol of Chinese subjugation. He would eventually cut it off.

After five months Lem was choking on the smallness of Chinatown and its thin air. He hopped a freight and headed into the mysteries of the Golden Mountain—it was such a big land. Lem worked small jobs in London, Montreal, Springhill, studying each place like an anthropologist, observing mood and culture, how Canadian men and women behaved. His Asian face was stared at curiously; there were so few Chinese. The road east had rarely been travelled; the Cantonese had stayed bunched into work gangs around jobs out west. But the jobs were almost ending. Lem hurried ahead, going all the way to the end of the track. He settled in Sydney before it was even a city and began washing clothes for the steel mill workers.

Lem Wong liked the cold slap of salt air and the friendliness of Cape Breton, when he could lift his head up from the job. Mostly he was buried alive in the laundry, working fourteen-hour days. He slept in a bed under the counter of the shop or on the ironing board. On

Fridays when the soiled laundry came piling in, Lem worked right through until Saturday night. His pay was $4 a week, less than half the salary of an unskilled white worker. The old Chinese would say they washed their laundry with tears.

Sometimes the blankness of exhaustion troubled Lem, and he'd force his mind awake. Sometimes exhaustion jabbed like a knife and his migraines throbbed all day. Lem often became blurry to himself, disappearing into his own hands. It was lonely work for a Chinese boy with no close friends, but his family had to be fed back in China. Pain was held in secretly—a body had to be willing to work and a face ready to smile. The steelworkers expected good service when they heaped their dirty laundry on Lem's counter.

Everything Lem did in the laundry he did by hand, scrubbing on the ribs of the washboard until his knuckles went soft. Lem worked six, sometimes seven days a week. The laundry charged a measly fifteen cents to wash and iron shirts, five cents for pairs of dirty socks, and eleven cents for collars. Detachable collars were the worst, small and stiff and slipping through the hands like fish. They absorbed most of the oil and dirt and Lem scrubbed them with brushes, bleached and boiled them, but they were hell to clean.

The job was never certain; the Chinese were always looking over their shoulders at the competition from the white-owned steam laundries. They were larger operations, grabbing the lucrative linen business from hotels and restaurants. An advertisement from the time told the story: "Is the Chinaman of today to be the Canadian of tomorrow? Let's hope not! Then patronize the Sanitary Steam Laundry."

It was a cutthroat trade and Chinese laundries got only the smallest, dirtiest part, servicing private homes and workingmen. It was their luck that a new nation was filling up with womenless men who needed clean laundry. Canada was bulging on a transient male population, as alone on the frontier as the Chinese. But gratitude was slim. Many of these journeymen, humiliated by their own work, lorded it over the Chinese, and sometimes over Lem. They called them chinks, Chinamen or Charlie. Lem didn't have enough hate to fight back. The words were stirred into the wash buckets along with the rest of the dirt.

Lem studied his customers, learning their manners, their forms of address. Remembering their names. He divined the goodness of their character even before they did. Sometimes he asked the men from Dominion Iron and Steel about their homes, sometimes they asked Lem about his. The men told him about the new blast furnaces at the mill and about the local miracles. It was a proud day for everyone in 1902 when Marconi sent a radio signal across the Atlantic from nearby Glace Bay. Lem's curiosity got the best of people; customers liked him.

Sometimes Lem journeyed out into the neighbourhoods, delivering his neatly wrapped brown paper laundry bundles. He'd peek through the doors of the little wooden houses, peering into the heart of their homes. It made him sure of what he wanted—a wife and house full of children. For five summers and numbing winters, Lem Wong saved his meagre earnings. Then he went back to China to find a wife.

Lem's mother was fierce about the marriage she'd arranged for Lem, but he refused. Perhaps it was Western living that made him stubborn. Lem had found another girl and couldn't be persuaded away from her. Finally his mother relented and Lem married Toye. Her feet were bound in the traditional way, toes curling beneath her feet.

Lem wasn't allowed to bring his wife back right away, public sentiment was against him. Ever since the end of the railway work, the country had been griping about the Chinese stealing jobs. Too many of them willing to work too cheap was the predictable lament. The government upped the Chinese head tax twice to $500, trying to keep them out. Then it tried to stop the flow of Chinese wives by putting impossible demands on their husbands. Lem couldn't bring Toye unless he was a merchant, and restaurants and laundries didn't count.

Lem bent over his washboard, saving more pennies, sending some home, eventually becoming a partner. He moved to London, Ontario, a quiet, wealthy town he remembered from his first train travels. He bought his own laundry, trying to make enough money to open another kind of business. The Golden Mountain was hard as hate. Toye gave birth to Lem's son in China and still Lem couldn't bring them over. Little Victor stumbled on his first steps while Lem opened a butter and egg shop. The shop failed and Victor learned to speak without ever hearing his father's voice. It took Lem Wong ten years to manoeuvre around Canadian law. Finally he succeeded with a fruit and vegetable shop. Sometime around 1912, Lem Wong brought his wife and nine-year-old Victor across the Pacific. He had spent over half his life in Canada, just trying to earn the right to a family. He was twenty-nine years old, ancient in his world.

Lem concentrated on finding a more lucrative business and on building his family. He wasn't alone. Chinese immigrants were fanning across Canada, pushed out of British Columbia by the hard shove of resentment and vicious mob attacks. They were starting communities all over Ontario and cramming into laundry jobs. Lem knew that work wouldn't last. The steam laundries and the arrival of immigrant women doing their own washing were already putting a dent in the trade. Lem decided on the restaurant business. It was 1914, a year of great expectations. As a new nation declared itself on the foreign battlefields of World War I, Lem Wong dared to reinvent himself. He opened Wong's Cafe.

The cafe was small, not an obvious place, but Lem made friends easily, greeting his customers and making them welcome. He built up his clientele on the manners he'd acquired out east, and on his business sense. Lem's family grew in the shadow of the cafe, eight children in all, each with an English name: Victor, Mary, Clara, Norm, George, Bill, Gretta and baby Esther. Four boys and four girls clustering together. There were a few Chinese in London, single men mostly, running stores on Clarence and King streets, and a few transients working for their meals at restaurants. But there weren't any other Chinese families to play with for a long time. The Wongs were alone, sons and daughters cut off from their parents' language and culture.

Lem never warned his children directly about discrimination; it wasn't a word he used. He told them only that they'd be noticed, and that they'd have to do a little better, as if it was an opportunity, not a curse. The children translated his words as an imperative to excel. Perhaps it's what their father meant.

Like many Chinese moving into Orange Ontario, Lem became a Presbyterian, an act of pragmatism as much as faith. A man's worth was measured by his devoutness and local allegiances. Lem nudged his children into Sunday school and choir—with so many Wongs, the joke was they could form their own choir. They fidgeted in their starched collars and Sunday dresses, as relieved as anyone when the services finished. But Christianity didn't eclipse Lem's first faith in Confucianism.

He had grown up on the ancient beliefs that stretched back to the Han Dynasty 206 B.C.—a code for social harmony in the brutal hierarchy of China. Confucius taught people to know their place and to act accordingly—women deferred to men, the young to the old, inferiors to their superiors. These were the tenets that made life bearable in the hostility of a new country. But fate wasn't absolute; there was mobility. Confucius taught that education could push people beyond their destiny. Lem was even more optimistic, believing that both men and women could develop their minds. He coaxed all his children beyond high school, offering his daughters encouragement that was rare for the time. The children groaned when their father told them fish was brain food. All through exams he fed them on seafood and bushels of apples.

These were his prizes, his well-formed, well-loved Canadian children, growing sturdily into the community, moving forward because their father knew they could. Only small minds made small opportunities, only the uneducated were doomed to repeat the past. Lem Wong pushed them into books and into team sports, and when he could, he took his family fishing or out on picnics. Toye would make food on an open fire, real egg rolls with green onions and meat rolled up in a paper-thin egg crepe. And the children would fly their kites—their beautiful hand-made kites, carefully assembled over weeks. Big dragons with long tails and butterflies with giant wings spread across the sky, and the wind carried the sounds of the children's squeals as they held the strings in their fists. Lem and Toye smiled beside them. Satisfied. Then the family would hurry home for three o'clock so Lem could get back to work.

Wong's Cafe was becoming well known. Lem had beautified the place, putting tablecloths and silver cutlery and finger bowls on the tables. His waiters all went to New York to learn how to hold trays over their heads. He built a dinner club on the second floor called the Rose Room and invited a soprano from the Grand Opera House to open it. Lem's inventiveness paid off. So did his memory. It confounded his children that Lem could recall the names of customers who'd been absent one or two years, greeting them like old friends. People delighted in Lem's warmth and good food. But resentment always hovered just outside the door.

Bruising stereotypes and punitive legislation were part of the bigger world Lem had to navigate, as inevitable as winter. In 1923 the Chinese Immigration Act barred all Chinese from entering Canada. Grudges hardened against Chinese who were already citizens, perhaps because they were competing in the restaurant business. The Chinese had managed to hoist themselves up from menial labour and laundries and by 1924, 9,000 worked in the trade as cooks, waiters and owners. The province retaliated with a law forbidding Lem to hire white women in his restaurant—the logic being that the Caucasian population needed protection from the corrupting influence of Chinese-Canadians. So much for market forces. It must have been wearing on Lem to have the details of his character reduced to cultural generalities, his efforts erased by caustic clichés that described the Chinese as wily, ruthless, sneaky, untrustworthy. And while London embraced Lem, it could never protect him from hateful perceptions lurking within smaller minds. Lem chose friendliness over resistance, softening himself instead of hardening. It took courage not to hear what was being said in the back of people's minds.

The law forced Lem to rely on men and on his family for labour. His daughters worked the cash and sometimes the kitchen while the boys did the heavier work. They all negotiated their sports and play schedules around their after-school job at the family restaurant. Lem's wife sewed the napkins and tablecloths, but she could never help him in the cafe.

Toye's feet had been badly maimed in the torturous rite that had been endured by Chinese women since the tenth century. Footbinding was a stamp of beauty and status, and ultimately obedience. Women could barely walk, let alone run away with bound feet. Not only was the foot crushed into smallness, it was shaped to look like a lotus flower. The most prized feet were only four or five inches long, the ever-tightening bandages curling girls' toes under their feet. Sometimes the toes rotted and fell off; always the pain had to be endured quietly. Lem got a doctor to unbind Toye's feet as much as he could. The children never saw them bare, but they winced watching their mother shuffle painfully. Who can guess the sorrow of a woman enduring so much agony only to arrive in a country where the effort seemed grotesque and barbaric? Her symbol of pride became a mark of shame. Toye flowered in the privacy of her family, but out in the world, she was always different. Lem and the children protected her fiercely.

Lem's mind continued to reach ahead, planning ways to tempt new customers. He was learning the subtleties of popular Canadian culture and the contradictions of its British and American impulses. The late 1920s was the great divide between Edwardian elegance and the longed for sensations of a faster, more Hollywood generation. Lem understood that. He built a dance floor and began bringing in big bands. London's own Guy Lombardo and his brothers are said to have started at Wong's Cafe. There were lots of imitators, too, at least eleven big bands in the area. Lem brought his teenage daughters to the auditions, using their Canadian sensibilities to help him choose who to hire. It was the wonder of Confucianism that Lem Wong, former washee man, could become an arbiter of cultural refinement.

Every Friday night the crowd held its breath and the Rose Room contracted with anticipation. Silverware shimmered, lights were lowered and the staff would try to tame their jittery nerves. There could be no rattling of dishes on Fridays. The master of ceremonies reached for the mike and said, "Good evening, ladies and gentlemen, direct from Wong's Cafe in London we bring you the music of Ken Solomon's Orchestra." Then he'd give the band a downbeat and they'd start in on their theme song. Radio station CJGC broadcast live from Wong's Cafe.

New Year's Eve was equally magical, each table booked long in advance. It was the kind of place every fella wanted to take his girl. The women wore corsages and the men had on their suits and ties. Lem greeted them at the top of the stairs, arms wide, and escorted them to their tables. He was a conjurer of dreams, able to satisfy the secret ache of every heart to live a little bit better.

Lem was never able to pay much, but he frequented the opera and the Grand Theatre, luring touring performers with a good dinner and maybe a few dollars. Once he even charmed the Dumbbells, the famous Vaudeville act, to come over and do a performance. Lem just had a way with people.

The laughter faded when the Great Depression came. It was bad for everyone and worse for the Chinese, who were last in line for jobs, and for the relief they would rarely ask for. Lem kept his fears out of the way of the children. They wouldn't know until they were grown how hard it had been.

The Hotel London came in about the same time, a big, posh place with dinner and dancing, dwarfing Wong's Cafe. The crowds thinned out and Lem had to cut back, relying on the children to help out more. Their schooling was still important but paying for it was harder. Sometimes the children couldn't get their results at the end of the year because their final fees weren't paid up. The school officers nodded from behind their counters, secretly affirming their passing marks, but unable to say anything out loud until accounts were settled.

The children made do through the lean years by sewing their clothes and crocheting hats to wear for church. They scavenged for watercress and hickory nuts to save on groceries, while Toye pulled vegetables from her garden. The family moved many times to cheaper places, finally settling in the cramped quarters above the cafe. Lem's migraines forced the household on tiptoe, and Toye shushed the children with a slap of her slipper. Lem didn't pause for self-pity; there were others he thought deserved it more.

Ragtag armies of single men were limping off the rails from the western dust bowl. Local fellows who couldn't get any welfare scrounged for food and work in those Dirty Thirties. Hungry, humiliated men found kindness at Wong's

Cafe. For years Lem worked with the Salvation Army to feed the poor at Christmas. He remembered the feel of an empty belly. The whole Wong family joined the effort.

On Christmas Lem cooked and served a full-course turkey dinner with nuts and pudding, insisting that his guests deserved the same menu as his paying customers. It was a lot of work—preparing the restaurant on Christmas Eve until three in the morning; getting up early to cook and do the final touches, serving dinner, then cleaning up for his regular Christmas dinner crowd. Who knows where those hundreds of men ended. Perhaps they remember the little Chinese man who offered them food so respectfully and lifted away their shame. For Lem it was simply a duty. He was just as generous with the Chinese. Lem was the first person called when something happened in the Asian community, day or night. When Chinese died, Lem helped arrange their funerals. He took people to the hospital, the doctor, to the lawyer's office to make up their wills. He was a special help to the ones who didn't speak English. There were no interpreters then and Lem did everything—citizenship papers, deeds, insurance certificates. Nor did he discriminate between the communities, not even as a father protecting the culture of his children. "You marry whomever you like," he told them again and again. "Find someone you can get along with." Family was important to Lem's sacred beliefs. And a good partner was essential, not his race. For Lem, the community was everyone.

As the Depression gulped men whole, Lem Wong managed to rebuild his business with brute will and work. His children thought of him as their phantom father, a man who appeared around eight at night to hear their stories and put them to bed, then disappeared into his work again. When the hard years finally receded into that place where nightmares live, Lem tried to retire. He had been working in Canada for over forty years. He sold Wong's Cafe in 1939, then turned around and bought the Melody in London East. His younger girls worked the soda bar during the summer. They didn't know a thing about making sodas and neither did Lem. He handed them a recipe book and told them they could do it if they tried. That was the way he was. Study, learn, do. And do it well because you would be noticed. It was a lesson that would last the girls a lifetime.

Then suddenly Canada declared war on Germany and a cold chill went up the spine of Canada's immigrants. It was a dangerous time. Lem was astonished at the hate at home and the hurt it caused. When Japanese-Canadians were sent inland, Lem met some sitting outside his church on the lawn. They weren't allowed inside or to sing in the choir. Lem spoke to the people at his church because he didn't think it was right, even if Japanese were supposed to be the enemy. They were all Christians and had to be treated equally.

Lem's sons returned from the war as full citizens and began their own lives and families while Lem tinkered with another restaurant. In 1947 the dreaded Chinese Immigration Act was repealed and the federal vote was extended to Asian Canadians. After fifty years in Canada, Lem Wong acquired the full rights of citizenship. He had managed to build a whole life without them. Lem slowly faded in the bright, ascending light of his children, proud to watch them succeed. They were his greatest legacy, imagined and worked for since the hard days as a laundryman in Cape Breton. Of his eight children, there were three doctors, a professor of chemistry, a draughtsman and a lawyer.

There was something completely unwavering about Lem and his determination to better himself. The humiliations meted out to Chinese-Canadians of his generation never made him bitter or twisted his personality out of shape. They only served to heighten his sense of principle. What mattered was character, duty and the pursuit of right over wrong. He used to say, "Take only the best of both worlds."

Lem and Toye Wong both lived to their ninety-eighth year, doted on by their children and grandchildren. Perhaps Canada had been the Golden Mountain after all.

Chinese Immigration History in Canada

Lem Wong arrived in Vancouver in 1897, part of a Chinese tradition of emigration that existed at the turn of the century. Seeking new opportunities overseas, the Chinese would send money back to support their relatives in China, holding to the hope that they would return home one day, prosperous.

From 1644 until the middle of nineteenth century, China had been an autonomous state under the imperial rule of the Ch'ing Dynasty. Eighteen thirty-nine marked the beginning of foreign domination, when the country fought unsuccessfully against Britain in the first of the Opium Wars. The Treaty of Nanking won England trading and territorial rights in China, and traditional government fractured. The land was tired and poverty was suddenly rampant. The population had exploded while farm yields remained stagnant. China's population nearly doubled between 1750 and 1850 from 200 or 250 million to about 410 million. Social and economic factors eventually led to the Taiping Rebellion, a peasant revolt between 1848 and 1865, in which twenty million people perished. Despite an imperial edict that imposed stiff penalties on those leaving the empire without a special permit, people started to seek a better living. And while the authority of a central government was restored by the 1870s, the rule of law wasn't. Banditry was high, and private armies became a way of life in rural China. For most Chinese emigrants, anything was better.

From the 1880s to the 1920s the Chinese in Canada were involved in the raw work of a fledgling industrial economy. Skilled or semiskilled Chinese laboured in the B.C. sawmills and salmon canneries. Others grew vegetables, cleared land or became peddlers, shopkeepers and restaurateurs. Unskilled but ambitious, Lem found work in the laundry trade.

Chinese people had been living in Vancouver long before Lem arrived. The first Chinese to settle in Canada were a small group of 50 artisans. They'd been contracted by Captain John Meares in 1788 to set up a trading post of otter pelts on Vancouver Island. It wasn't until 1858 that the next wave of Chinese came to Canada, pulled by the lure of the gold rush in the Fraser River Valley. The first Chinese community in Canada was formed in Barkerville, British Columbia. By 1860 the Chinese population of Vancouver Island and British Columbia was 6,000.

This wave of Chinese immigrants was made up of young peasants, mostly from South China. Rural poverty and political unrest in their homeland pushed them to emigrate. In the 1870s and 1880s they were followed by another wave of young peasant migrants who came to build the Canadian Pacific Railway through the Rockies. Fifteen thousand Chinese labourers worked on the British Columbia section of the CPR, completing it in 1885. Their meagre pay of $1 a day was half the wage of white labourers, and saved the CPR an estimated $3 million to $5 million in construction costs. However, landslides and careless dynamite blasts killed many Chinese labourers who were enlisted for the most dangerous work. It's said that one Chinese worker died for every mile of the railway. History blurs the tragedy—no records were kept at the time. But recent research puts the number closer to three Chinese workers for every mile.

After the railway jobs dried up, Chinese were shunned and left to fend for themselves. Despite this, Chinese communities managed to develop across the entire country. Entrepreneurial and hard-working, the Chinese reinvented themselves according to market forces. When the railway work was over in 1885 only about five percent of Chinese worked in the laundries, but they steadily moved into service jobs. By 1921, more than thirty percent were working in laundries and restaurants; ten years later it was forty percent. Then, as the demand for hand laundry declined, Chinese workers concentrated in the restaurant business. There were 1,400 Chinese laundrymen in 1924, and 9,000 in restaurants.

Lem followed the shape of opportunity, travelling all the way to the Atlantic to wash clothes in Sydney, then starting his own cafe in London. When he'd saved enough money to find a Chinese wife, it took him years to bring her to Canada.

Canadian policy was aimed at stopping Asian immigration after the building of the railway. The government imposed harsh head taxes, effectively preventing Chinese women from immigrating and, Chinese workers.

Overcoming Obstacles

Since 1885, Chinese immigrants like Lem Wong had been forced to pay an "entry" or "head" tax of $100 upon entering Canada. By the turn of the century Asian immigration was further restricted by the federal government.

In 1902 the government set up a Royal Commission on Chinese and Japanese Immigration. The commission reported that Asians were "unfit for full citizenship... obnoxious to a free community and dangerous to the state."

Acting on the report, Parliament passed legislation in 1903 raising the head tax to $500. Not surprisingly, Chinese immigration the following year dropped to 8 people from 4,719 the year before. But even these laws couldn't stop the human urge for betterment. As the number of Chinese immigrants began increasing again, the Canadian government passed the Chinese Exclusion Act, virtually eliminating Chinese immigration. The date of its passage, July 1, 1923, became known to the Canadian Chinese as "Humiliation Day." For many years the Chinese refused to observe Canada Day which is celebrated on the same date.

Bruising prejudices and stereotypes surrounded Chinese-Canadians at the time. Other Canadians regarded overcrowded Chinese living quarters as unsanitary and disease-infested, and they resented the willingness of the Chinese to work long and hard for low wages.

For Lem Wong, the years and years of working in the laundry trade and as a vegetable and poultry merchant gradually paid off. But when he ventured into his own restaurant business, he was still limited by punitive legislation. It was illegal for Chinese men to employ white women because of a provincial law designed to protect the white population from "corruption" by Chinese-Canadians.

In 1947, discriminatory legislation against the Chinese finally began to be repealed and Chinese-Canadians were granted the right to vote. But restrictions on Chinese immigration were not entirely removed until 1967.

The Chinese-Canadian Legacy

By 1993 about 700,000 people of Chinese ancestry were living in Canada. Much of the later immigration was from Hong Kong. From 1983 to 1993, 166,487 Hong Kong immigrants settled in Canada, perhaps in anticipation of the island's return to Chinese control in 1997, after being a British colony for over a century.

Since 1900 most Chinese immigrants have settled in urban centres. Over sixty-eight percent of Chinese-Canadians currently live in Toronto and Vancouver.

Through to the 1980s, Chinese-Canadians were mainly employed in the service industries. But by the 1990s they were moving into many fields, including the arts, journalism and politics, professions such as law and medicine, as well as traditional careers in education, science and business.

One of the greatest contributions of Chinese immigrants to Canada has been investment in the Canadian economy. One of the major investors has been Li Ka-shing, who bought Husky Oil and Gas in Alberta in 1987 and the Expo 86 lands for development as Pacific Place in Vancouver in 1988. Both his sons, Richard and Victor, are Canadian citizens.

Lem Wong's sons, Bill, George and Norman, served in WW II and wore their Canadian uniforms proudly.

China and Canada, along with the United States and Britain, had become wartime allies against Japan. And the service of Chinese-Canadians went a long way in changing the nativistic sentiments of many Canadians. Suddenly the faces of Chinese-Canadians were those of heroes.

In 1945, Chinese-Canadians who had fought for Canada in either world war were given the right to vote, two years before the rest of their community. In 1947 all Chinese-Canadians were enfranchised and the anti-Chinese immigration law of 1923 was finally repealed. After the war, Canadian attitudes were changing. The atrocities at Auschwitz and Buchenwald haunted the world and opened minds to the horrors of prejudice.

For Lem Wong, the humiliations that had been meted out to Chinese-Canadians of his generation never seemed to make him bitter. He persevered with a heightened sense of principle. The legacy he left his children was that it didn't really matter whether something was Chinese or Western. What mattered to him was what was right or wrong. As Lem himself used to say, "You should only take the best of both worlds."

Sources

The Canadian Encyclopedia, World Edition. McClelland & Stewart, Toronto, 1998.

Chinatowns: Towns Within Cities in Canada, David Chuenyan Lai. University of British Columbia Press, Vancouver, 1988.

The Chinese in Canada, Peter S. Li. Oxford University Press, Toronto, 1988.

The Fitzhenry & Whiteside Book of Canadian Facts & Dates, Jay Myers. Fitzhenry & Whiteside, Richmond Hill, 1991.

From China to Canada: A History of the Chinese Communities in Canada, Harry Con, Ronald J. Con, Graham Johnson, Edgar Wickberg and William E. Willmott; Edgar Wickberg, editor. McClelland & Stewart, Toronto, 1982.

Gold Mountain: the Chinese in the New World, Anthony B. Chan. New Star Books,Vancouver, 1983.

The Lotus Lovers: The *Complete History of the Curious Erotic Custom of Footbinding in China,* Howard S. Levy. Prometheus Books, Buffalo, 1992.

The Road Chosen, directed by Keith Lock. White Pine Pictures, Toronto, 1998.

Struggle and Hope: The Story of Chinese Canadians, Paul Yee. Umbrella Press, Toronto, 1996.

Martha Purdy Bl

Chapter Seven
First Lady of the Yukon: Martha Purdy Black

Canada and the World in 1898

In August, the Yukon Territory is created by an act of Parliament.

New Westminister, B.C., is destroyed by fire.

Two-cent Imperial postage is introduced; one stamp will ensure the delivery of letters anywhere in the British Empire.

The Spanish-American War rages.

In France, Pierre and Marie Curie discover radium, which later revolutionizes cancer treatment.

H.G. Wells writes *War of the Worlds,* his famous science-fiction story about an invasion of martians.

Author and photographer Lewis Carroll, best known for *Alice's Adventures in Wonderland,* dies.

Pancake mix, chewing gum, aluminum kitchen utensils, mimeograph machines, phonographs, picture postcards, Coca-Cola and flush toilets become available in the 1890s.

Martha Louise Munger was five years old when the great Chicago fire of 1871 razed her city. Fire turned the sky red and blistered the homes of 100,000 people. The Munger family raced from the flames, barely able to breathe. Throats and eyes burned and the known world disappeared. It was a sudden tearing away from the protective order of her life, a first glimpse at other expressions on the human face. It was both horrible and exhilarating.

Martha's family escaped to the sandy banks of Lake Michigan, camping in the open with thousands of others. Martha baked potatoes for the first time over a fire. Later the family moved into tents, waiting for their grand home and laundry business to be rebuilt. Martha liked the clearness of that time, the direct sensation of air on her skin, the October cold in her nose, the mix of humanity and the kindness of strangers. It was her first memory and it scratched deeply against the grain of her upbringing.

Martha Louise was a Daughter of the American Revolution; the ninth generation of American-born Mungers. Her people included Button Gwinett, one of the signers of the Declaration of Independence. Martha Louise was the inheritor of strong blood and independent thinking; awkward strengths for a rich girl growing up in the second half of the nineteenth century. She was born restless and chafed under the stern gaze of upper-class Chicago society. High spirits and intelligence made her an uneasy fit. When her grandparents refused to let her on a hot air balloon at the circus, Martha fished a quarter out of her own pocket and snuck aboard. The spanking that followed brought no obvious change in her temperament.

Martha Louise's home was full of noise and loving, well-informed people. But always there was the sharp eye of her father and his cautions against immodesty. When she boasted that she could collect 100 four-leaf clovers, her father promised $1 for every one she picked, hoping to embarrass her. Fifty dollars later, Mr. Munger begged out of the contract.

Martha Louise bobbed through private school, learning the social graces of curtseying, elocution, fine needlework and baking lemon cream pies. But her passions were immediate and Martha stumbled blindly over rules. Teachers complained so often that the Mungers pulled her out and sent Martha to the nuns for a convent education. Five years later Martha graduated, the only student who didn't receive a favourable conduct wreath. What she did get was a bouquet of calla lilies from the immensely marriageable Will Purdy.

Martha Louise was introduced to society in a flutter of pink silk and lace in the fall of 1885. For months afterward, she was carried on a current of parties and social diversions. The handsome Will Purdy, son of a railway president, was one of the approved boys in the frantic, last season of husband finding. In August of 1887, he married Martha Louise and the Purdys settled into a twenty-room suburban home outside Chicago, a gift from Father Munger. Marriage brought sudden freedom—for the first time in her life, Martha Louise was able to go to the local shops unchaperoned.

Within a year, Martha gave birth to her first son, Warren; then she and Will hurtled into the Gay Nineties. The Purdys were part of a new generation of well-to-do—prosperous, urbane, with a swirl of friends and distractions. Martha Louise hoisted up her skirts and careened around with Will on their bicycle built for two. Nice wives weren't supposed to know about low life, but Martha went downtown anyway, taking a peak at the fancy whores in paint and powder, and attending Turkish baths and daring chorus shows. But the flush of meaning and romance didn't last. Will's work pulled him away from Martha and their second son, Donald, began school. Martha raised money for the poor, and for the Cuban Rebellion of 1895 but a brooding dullness strangled her. At thirty years old, Martha Louise was bored stupid. She visited an East Indian palmist to amuse herself and his prediction was startling: "You are leaving this country within a year. You will travel far. You will face danger, privation and sorrow. Although you are going to a foreign land, you will be among English-speaking people, and will never have to learn to speak another language. You will have another child, a girl, or an unusually devoted son."

Across the country, a grizzled gang of miners poured off the *Excelsior* steamship in San Francisco, breathless with tales of a northern bonanza. The summer before, three prospectors had struck gold in Rabbit Creek, near the Klondike river. Now the story was inching across the continent. "Gold by the ton, by the bagful, nuggets as big as eggs, dust as thick as carpets." The stampede was on.

When news hit Chicago, it climbed up the spine of every dreamer, including Will Purdy. For men and fools perched at the end of a century, the gold rush was a last claim on the untamed self, the fierce final pull on masculinity from the dullness of mechanized life. And a chance to get rich quick. Will formed a partnership with a friend and both men called on their fathers to bankroll them. Martha Louise was infected, too, ears straining as the men made plans to cross the north. It was uncertainty that thrilled her, the same sudden sensation she felt camping as a child at Lake Michigan. Martha Louise had to get to the Klondike.

Martha's parents volunteered to take care of her children, but it was her husband and father-in-law she had to convince. Luck intervened. One of Father Purdy's employees arrived with a fantastic story about a dead uncle bequeathing his family $1 million in Klondike gold. Mr. Lambert wanted someone to bring the gold back and offered to pay fifty percent. The men decided it was a job for Martha Louise. It was settled—she was going to the Klondike. Will left first, to organize provisions in Seattle, before heading up to Dawson.

There were hard moments before going, a flagging of resolve as Martha Louise said goodbye to her boys. They were so little. As she steadied herself to leave, her brother George, who'd been wavering for weeks, decided to come along. They set off for Seattle to meet Will, but he'd been waylaid on business in San Francisco. Worse, Will Purdy had changed his mind. He wrote to Martha about awful rumours he'd heard—deprivation and robberies along the northern trail. Will thought they should head to the Sandwich Islands—Hawaii. Or maybe Martha should leave Seattle and go back home.

Martha Louise was white with fury, afraid too, of what her own mind was hatching. Something steely welled up inside her, a certainty that neither terror nor social disapproval could stifle. She wasn't going to burrow back into the boredom of Chicago. She was going to the Klondike with or without Will Purdy. George was appalled. Martha would later recall his reaction: "He threatened to send for Father to make me go home. I coaxed, pleaded, cajoled. I said I would go alone. I was tired of the monotonous round of the society life of Chicago....This was an opportunity to seek and claim my fortune....I'd never ask a thing of him again."

George gave in, agreeing to tell their father only after they'd sailed.

The Seattle docks were humming with the raw nerve of human hope that June of 1898, every shape of man and whim exposed. Class distinctions faded in the sameness of trail clothes; gentlemen shoved against rogues and soft-skinned boys against hard-boiled prospectors. Martha and George elbowed their way to the *Utopia*, a broken-down tub where Martha paid $120 for the luxury of a stateroom and a triple berth. On June 23 they set out for Dyea, just past Skagway, Alaska. It was the end of privilege as Martha had known it.

Martha Louise Purdy was astonished to find she was sharing her stateroom—a small-time gambler, his girlfriend and another woman of low repute called Birdie stared back at her casually, as if sharing a room with a man was the most normal thing in the world. Martha's tears weren't enough; it was a take-it-or-leave-it situation. In the morning, she accepted the gambler's proffered cup of coffee and looked less sourly on Birdie. Martha Louise had learned her first hard lessons in Yukon survival—the necessity of compromise and the suspension of judgement, though it wasn't so easy stepping over the drunken gamblers sleeping on the decks, or the animals leaning over the sides.

For seven days the *Utopia* steamed along the inland passage, nosing up the rocky edges of British Columbia and Alaska. Martha saw icebergs for the first time, and dolphins and orca whales. Small Indian villages blinked from shore. Night began to disappear and by Skagway it was continual day. Martha and George steamed on to Dyea, the small, sudden city of tents that had sprung up by a Tlingit native village and trading post. In the distance was the hard shoulder of the Chilkoot Pass: "The worst trail this side of hell." Martha's supplies were tossed onto shore. As she watched the *Utopia* pull away, she refused to be afraid. A million dollars in gold lay ahead, in a north already trampled by thousands of other dreamers.

Martha's destination was Dawson City, 430 miles away. Most of the travelling could be done by boat, starting at Lake Bennett. But to get there, she had to hike forty miles over the mountains. There were two ways to do it. The White Pass Trail was longer, but easier for pack animals carrying supplies. Still, so many horses died it was known as Dead Horse Trail. Martha and George decided on the Chilkoot Pass.

The Chilkoot was an old Indian trail. The Tlingit said there was a curse on trying to cross it in summer, but for $1,000 an outfit, they carried up packs for the gold diggers. It was the law of the north that everyone bring a year's supply of food, enforced by Sam Steele, the superintendent of the North-West Mounted Police. The year before had been disastrous; only half the miners had made it out before winter. The ones left behind weren't prepared and many starved or froze to death. Sam Steele wasn't going to let that happen again, no matter how many spines groaned under the weight of their supplies.

Martha Louise and her brother hired packers to pull their tons of supplies over the pass to Lake Bennett. They left Dyea on July 12, following an easy wagon road for five or six miles. Martha was stylish in her long skirts and walking stick, a strangely feathered bird in the pack of bearded, grunting men. As the trail became rockier, she scrambled over stones and boulders, through miles of valley, barren as tundra. Martha's feet began to ache and, as the ground sloped upward, there were signs of harder luck. Dead horses that had fallen down the mountainside were mangled in heaps; discarded supplies lay mute as tombstones.

By day's end, Martha staggered into the town of Sheep Camp at the foot of the pass—a flimsy street with a single shack called the Grand Pacific Hotel. Three months earlier an avalanche had swept through, crushing sixty people. Today they were pulling bodies from the rubble and burying them properly. Martha Louise folded into the welcome of a hot meal and a bed of straw, dreaming the dream of the dead. Tomorrow would be her turn to face the Chilkoot.

The day started crisp and clean. Martha twisted her head skyward to the thin black line of men and animals moving single file over icy rock. It was a 3,000-foot climb, almost straight up. Martha Louise stepped into line at the bottom and moved slowly through the morning, heaving herself up with her stick. Men warned her not to look down; they offered their arms, hands, to hoist her forward. As the trail got steeper, the beating sun made the edges soggy—there was no place to find a foothold. The heat hurt and Martha pulled off her sealskin jacket. Her boned corset jabbed into her ribs, her feet tangled in the folds of her corduroy skirt. She gulped in the thin air, wanting to fall to the side, to rest. But Martha was wedged into the line of climbers, and there was nowhere to fall except down.

"Cheer up, Polly," George called out. "Only 100 feet to go now." Martha lurched forward, tumbling into a crack of rock. It was a lucky fall, but something sharp ripped through her boot, gashing her shin. Martha Louise rolled into a ball and started to weep. Man after man stopped to offer help and George too tried to soothe his sister, but she wouldn't quit crying. "For God's sake, Polly, buck up and be a man. Have some style and move on!"

Exhausted and embarrassed, Martha Louise Purdy yanked herself up by sheer force of pride and walked the last few feet to the summit. Finally, the cold, white top of the world and the beginning of Canada. Only the wind cut through Martha's numbness, and the surprising good manners of the North-West Mounted Police. The Canadians were civil and offered a sturdy assurance of law and order. Martha passed through customs and then headed down the other side.

The nearest town was two miles down, and Lake Bennett two miles after that. Those last steps were unexpected and excruciating. Martha teetered on wobbly legs, braking herself against gravity. She stumbled over scrub bush, bleeding from hands and feet. There was only Martha's instinct left, and the unintelligible mutterings of fatigue. George had to carry his sister the last mile into Lindeman where Martha sank into a canvas cot at the Tacoma Hotel. Her mind twitched on a single, satisfying thought. Martha Louise Purdy had walked over the Chilkoot Pass. God, that *was* something:

> As my senses slipped away into the unconsciousness of that deep sleep of exhaustion, there surged through me a thrill of satisfaction. I had actually walked over the Chilkoot Pass!...I would never do it again, knowing now what it meant....Not for all the gold in the Klondyke....And yet, knowing now what it meant, would I miss it...no, never!...Not even for all the gold in the world!

It took a couple of days for Martha's body to unclench, for her eyes to adjust to the land's beauty. For two wonderful weeks she settled into a cabin with her brother, waiting for her baggage to get to Lake Bennett. Travellers from all over the world moved up and down the mountains, bringing news and advice. It was a time of easy friendships with adversity binding the most unlikely. Campfires spilled red light on the faces of hard-made men, and they strangled out their songs—"My Darling Clementine," "A Bicycle Built for Two," "Sweet Rosie O'Grady." Martha Louise curled like a child into those nights, like her five-year-old self on the banks of Lake Michigan, assured of the goodness of strangers.

There were bears, too, pawing at the camp food at night. Martha Louise demanded to sleep with a loaded gun, and the men laughed, saying she'd probably point the wrong end. It gave her something to prove. When she heard a rustling a few nights later, she got her gun, barrel end out, and crept to the window. Something clawed up her sleeve and inside her nightgown. Martha Louise screamed and screamed and the whole camp rushed in. For days afterwards the old-timers had something to chew on besides their tobacco. Martha Louise was being woven into the story of the north.

When Martha's supplies finally arrived at Lake Bennett, she and George loaded them onto a boat heading toward Dawson. It took them a day to make the forty miles to Caribou Crossing, and another one to reach Lake Tagish, where the North-West Mounted Police kept a post. Like every other boat, theirs was stopped and searched for liquor. Martha's fellow passengers were particularly considerate of her comfort, building a little deck seat for Martha out of boxes and blankets. Later she learned that the boxes were hiding a couple of cases of whisky.

It took twelve days for the boat to sail to Dawson. The first part was the worst, a white-knuckled rush through Miles Canyon and the White Horse Rapids, where people were too often slammed to their deaths. The Yukon River was gentler and always there was a crowd of other boats—canoes, dories—men clinging to anything that floated. At night everyone camped on shore, dodging mosquitoes and rubbing themselves madly with eucalyptus oil. One afternoon Martha and her brother stumbled on a crew of wary-eyed New Zealand miners who'd just struck gold by a creek. The men hunched away from them, afraid their unrecorded claim would be filched in the raw scrabble for gold. As Martha dangled warm food their way, the men's tongues loosened. They said Martha's hardtack and apple dumpling was the best meal they'd had since leaving home. They let Martha christen the creek "Excelsior," a name that would outlive her. Then she and George staked their own first claim. Two days later they made it to Dawson.

Dawson was a mob scene, a whooping, slouching, lopsided place crammed with 30,000 people, an assault on Victorian senses. Almost every other building was a dance hall, saloon or hotel, with names like the Floradora, Northern, Monte Carlo, Sourdough, Can Can. There were lots more women here, too, painted ones with loose-hipped, swaggering gaits and gold-toothed grins. Every courtesy was abbreviated, every impulse acted on in the hot flush of winning and losing. Dawson was a money-talking, money-grubbing town, and everything was for sale. Even gambling and prostitution were legal, except on Sundays. The Lord's Day was strictly enforced by the North-West Mounted Police; so were the gun laws. There wasn't much shooting in the Canadian North. Much to the surprise of the Americans, revolvers required a licence.

Martha and George tramped through town looking for a space to set up a tent or cabin, but all the good lots were picked clean. They crossed the Klondike River and built a one-room cabin on the hillside above Lousetown—

"The lousiest place on God's earth, for any day the lice might walk away with them buildins." George shaped furniture out of tree trunks, twigs and packing boxes, while Martha uncrated her linen tablecloths and silver cutlery. She was nesting furiously, making curtains and pinning blankets to walls to cheer up the place. Despite her domesticity, she was also filling up her mouth with the language of the north. George was horrified. "What will people think of you?" he admonished. "Think of me! If I get my half-million I won't give a damn; and if I don't, then they won't give a damn for me!"

George went staking claims on the Excelsior, as Martha headed out to the gold commissioner's office to dig out Lambert's records and her $1 million in gold. The officials weren't eager to hand over their papers, so Martha waited them out with her perfect manners. Their books were cooked—scratched-up ledgers and cancelled claims, whole pages snipped out and repasted with other names. There was no registration claim for Lambert, only the fact that he had existed and died.

Martha spent weeks chasing down small leads and the threads of mumbled conversations. There was no trace of a gravestone or of the witnesses who'd signed Lambert's will. Martha greased many palms along the way, but money ran low and she was forced to give up. There was no half-million in gold for Martha Louise.

By now the Yukon was more than just a place in the imagination; it was officially declared a territory, through an Act of Parliament, with a commissioner and an appointed territorial council of ten. The commissioner was James Morrow Walsh, the famous North-West Mounted Police inspector who'd negotiated peace with Sitting Bull in 1876 when he'd escaped into Canada after the Battle of Wounded Knee. But Martha Louise was oblivious to politics. August was turning quickly into autumn and bringing the last orange heat of Indian Summer. Panic crept through Dawson, and miners made a last frantic rush on the claims office. The *Klondyke Nugget* warned the newcomers to get on out if they weren't prepared for a hard winter. People sold off their outfits and hurried onto boats. Martha began thinking of getting out too.

Martha Louise had grown pale over the months. Ever since the Chilkoot she'd been trying to convince herself that her body's changes had to do with the climate. But by September there was no denying the truth—she was pregnant, a parting gift from Will. She couldn't leave now; she'd never make it over the pass. Martha kept hold of her secret until the last boat was gone, knowing the worry it would bring. When she finally told George, he blubbered that his father would never forgive him. It was male helplessness that made women like Martha more resolute.

As winter descended, the nights grew so long that day disappeared. The Yukon cold of seventy below stopped the world from getting in. Martha settled into her pregnancy, cooking and sewing by candlelight. She and George played checkers at night on a homemade board. Martha Louise stung with homesickness for her other two boys, and for the safety of Chicago life. She refused to sing "Home Sweet Home," and pulled down the photographs of her parents and children because they made her sad. She didn't write to them about the baby when the last ships had been going—there was nothing they could do.

Martha's body craved fruits and vegetables, but she and George began rationing themselves to a diet of cornmeal mush and tea. There was nothing fresh to eat, no more butter or sugar. Martha was afraid of hunger. She couldn't afford the $16 for a gallon of milk, let alone the $1,000 for a hospital bed. Father Judge, the priest who ran the hospital, offered Martha credit until ice broke and the boats came in with money. Martha refused, deciding to have the baby at home rather than being in debt. But she was scared; her other babies had been born in the sanitized wards of Chicago hospitals. She'd never had a baby alone.

Word spread through Dawson that a child was on the way, and it pulled at the goodness in every pioneer. Men and women poked their frozen faces through Martha's door, offering whatever they could. Stampeders brought pots of homemade jam, tablecloths to sew into baby dresses and treats for Christmas dinner. It was an infectious jubilance they brought to Martha, and a courage to face what lay ahead.

The baby came early. Martha Louise was attended by a one-armed man with a hook for a hand and an old sea captain. They were gentle with Martha, the one man wrapping his hook in cotton. Martha Louise named the baby Lyman, for her grandfather. The men of the camp called him "Little Chechako," a native word meaning newcomer, or do-nothing. They scurried around Martha, proving their usefulness by tending fires and baking bread. Every sort of man called to pay his respects, bearing gifts of chocolate and moose meat, olive oil, gold nuggets, gold dust. They were the wise men and they told Martha stories about their children far away. They wanted to touch her boy, to remember the feel of their own babies' toes and downy backs, to smell the bready scent of an infant. Their raw hands stroked him carefully. It was a tenderness that marked Martha's heart for a lifetime. Finally she wrote home to her parents.

> February 10, 1899: On Tuesday, at noon, January 31st, my third son was born, and I welcomed him with delight. He weighs nine pounds, and is as hale as hearty as any baby born under happier conditions....I am enclosing a curl of his hair. Embrace my other little ones for me. Tell them about their new little brother, and be ready to welcome the wanderers.

As winter loosened its grip and daylight lengthened, Martha Louise floated on the euphoria of motherhood, fussing over Lyman. She carried him to the river and watched the boats returning with shipments of fresh food and a new crop of stampeders. Surviving the winter made Martha one of the old-timers, a "sourdough." She moved around Dawson with a sense of ownership and belonging—these were her people now, her place. The winter had erased the last of her upper-class pretensions, taught her about the decency of working men and women. Even the dance-hall girls found a place in Martha's heart and the percentage girls plying their charms so the men would buy drinks. It seemed a lifetime ago that she'd turned up her nose at Birdie on board the *Utopia*. Martha hated to see the women so looked down on.

Even before Martha had arrived, Dawson was becoming more permanent and a little more respectable. She could sense it dividing along old class lines. Martha didn't like it. She walked by Government House detesting its exclusiveness, how only the well-to-do were invited in. If she were running the show, she'd pull the doors wide open to the real citizens of the Yukon—the miners, prospectors and all the others who'd built the place. But the lowly born had their own revenge—living big. And Martha loved their noise.

> July 4, 1899: It is a gala day in Dawson, and the Canadians are seemingly delighted to help us celebrate our national holiday as we were to join with them on Dominion Day (July 1). In fact, the celebration has been a continued spree, the all-time daylight making many think there is no bedtime.

The fourth of July was announced with a blast of gunshot, one minute after midnight, and 10,000 Americans and Canadians marched together, voices zigzagging between "My Country 'Tis of Thee" and "God Save the Queen." Dogs ran for cover and revelers ran for liquor. It was the last celebration Martha attended that year.

Near the end of July, Martha's father suddenly arrived in Dawson, announcing that he'd come to fetch his daughter home. Martha couldn't really argue—she was penniless. Her claims hadn't come in and she had a new baby to raise. Mr. Munger surveyed the cabin sourly, blaming Martha's husband for her poverty. "I cannot understand any man allowing his wife to go alone on such a trip as this, not even accepting his legal responsibility." It was on the grounds of abandonment that Mr. Munger would later encourage his daughter to sue for divorce. Now he only wanted to get her home. Martha Louise was cornered by daughterly duty and economic necessity. But she made her father promise that if gold came in on her Excelsior claim, she could come right back. Her father consented, forgetting perhaps about his daughter's uncanny ability to win her wagers.

A few weeks later Martha was rushing into the arms of her two little boys, her nose burrowing into their smell. They had grown plenty after a whole year's absence. The Munger home soothed Martha at first—no more worry over the price of milk, or the scarcity of food. She could divorce Will and live respectably with her children on her father's wealth. But the Yukon hovered at the seam between her night and day dreams; the hum of its rivers and winds moved between her thoughts, as internal as breath. All winter she fidgeted and the house filled up with her parents' worried whispers. Martha was disappearing. When George finally sent word that their claim had struck gold, Martha Louise set off to the Klondike. She left the baby and Donald at home and brought twelve-year-old Warren.

Martha didn't have to claw up the Chilkoot this time—by 1900 there was a new train running to Lake Bennett. Nor was she the flimsy *chechako* flinching at the North's surprises. She carried the assurance of her own money and her own plans. Martha Louise intended to make the Yukon home. She bought into a partnership at a mining camp outside Dawson. Sixteen men were hired and Martha did all the cooking while Warren attended school. It was hard and constant work. Always there was the wordless instinct of her heart, the ache for her other children.

The following year Martha's parents arrived with Donald and Lyman, the missing parts of her jigsaw puzzle life. The whole family nestled into a handsome, six-room cabin they called Mill Lodge and set up a couple of sawmills on the bank of the Klondike river. A few months later the Mungers took Warren back to school in the States, where he would stay, and Martha was left to run the mills alone. It was a rare role for a woman, one Martha Louise had to fill up fiercely. Some of the men didn't like being "run by a skirt," especially a successful skirt.

At first Martha ignored the grumblings, not sure of her authority. She kept to her work—seventeen hours a day mothering two boys, running the mill and two mill crews, as well as taking over the sales end because her salesman turned out to be a drunk. Deliberate sabotage yanked her into action. The foreman was a lout, threatening to quit and to take the whole crew with him. Martha shrugged them all off. For three days she and nine-year-old Donald worked the machines by themselves until Martha signed up a whole new crew.

The Yukon was growing up around Martha. The territory was finally granted the right to elect a member to the Dominion Parliament in Ottawa. Dawson was shaking off its frontier dust, slapping on a new coat of big city polish. The whoops of prospectors and the all-night parties grew fainter. Martha still caught the strains of the different nationalities singing their songs around Dawson—the Irish crooning Killarney, the Scots bellowing Loch Lomond, the French chanting Alouette, but the Klondike days were fading into memory. At the intersection between old and new Dawson was the bitter argument about letting dance hall-girls into the swanky new ice rink. Tolerance won out, but with the stern proviso that any girl caught smoking or using profane language would have her pass revoked. Dawson was cleaning up its act.

Martha Louise had come full circle. The girl who'd escaped her class privilege in Chicago was becoming one of the leading citizens of the new Dawson. Martha Louise, a lady by birth, a stampeder by inclination, was now a founding businesswoman. The early years of the new century hurried past Martha as she set fingerbone to grindstone. Her first claims turned out to be real pay dirt and the sawmills made her big money. Martha Louise could now afford to order fine furniture from the Eaton's catalogue; she bought beautiful clothes and a yearly gown from Madame Aubert in Paris. While Warren attended American private schools, Donald and Lyman were planted in public school, firmly Canadian. Wealth didn't turn Martha Louise away from her first constituency—the raw and ragged ones who had come north to lay claim to a dream. Her heart remained tender to the working girls and their hard-luck stories. When one of the local landladies of a boozy boardinghouse needed help, she ran to Martha. The landlady's mother and son were coming north and she was desperate for a respectable front.

"Saturday and Sunday are apt to be wild days at my place," the woman pleaded. "Will you help me and ask them to visit you weekends? I'll pay you anything you want." Martha watched the whole world's misery in the woman's eyes.

"Why not rent one of my mill cabins for your mother and son. Your little fellow can play with my boys and I'll see your mother has plenty to do over the weekend."

"God bless you, God bless you," the woman spluttered, tears splashing down her face.

There still weren't many women in the north, fewer still with nice homes to entertain. Martha Louise was inundated with marriage proposals by the week. Then along came George Black, a New Brunswick lawyer. Within two weeks of meeting Martha, he too proposed. It took two years for Martha Louise to make up her mind. George worked on her through the boys—taking them on canoe and hiking trips, teaching them photography. She finally married George in August 1904 and became Mrs. Black—an Anglican, a Conservative and a British imperialist, like her husband. Lyman took George's last name, too.

The Blacks straddled all the different Yukons, fitting as easily into the rugged world of bear hunting and canoeing as into Dawson's burgeoning aristocracy. George headed into Conservative politics and was elected to the Yukon Council three times. Martha followed him into the hinterlands, paddling and portaging for days to reach isolated voters. In 1912 George accepted an appointment as the seventh commissioner of the Yukon Territory. Donald, Lyman, George and Martha moved out of Mill Lodge and took up residence in Government House. For Martha Louise, it was a chance to avenge her people's snubbing, the miners and workingmen and women. She flung open the doors of Government House to everybody, transforming the place into a house of the people. There was all kinds of noise and bent feelings as the respectable and less respectable collided in the banquet halls. Martha negotiated for all of them, balancing formality with spontaneity. When one old sourdough friend said he was bringing the missus to an event, Martha made sure it was his real wife. He'd already introduced her to several wives already.

In August of 1914 the Blacks were entertaining in Dawson's one moving-picture house when a telegram was handed to George—England was at war with Germany. The territory heaved into action and George resigned as commissioner and enlisted. He organized a Yukon Infantry Company and was appointed captain. One of the first to join his company was Lyman. Martha's other son, Warren, commanded a troop ship, while Donald graduated from Stanford and joined up with the Americans. All Martha's men were in service; her first and only urge was to follow them. As usual, her determination was unstoppable. Martha enlisted everyone's help, even Prime Minister Robert Borden's, to get permission to travel with her family. No one objected as long as the transportation commander in Halifax, General Bigger, consented. Bigger was evasive: "But Mrs. Black, you wouldn't want to be the only woman on board a ship of 2,000 men, would you?" She responded, "General Bigger, I walked over the Chilkoot Pass with thousands of men and not one wanted to elope with me." An hour before the ship left, Martha found out she was going. The general had waited to talk to George, making sure he really did want his wife to go.

The Yukon Infantry Company, 275 strong, left Dawson on the SS *Casca* on October 16, 1916. Martha Louise Black was the only woman aboard. Sergeant Barwell wrote a small poem to honour her departure.

We have stolen Mrs. Black, and we will not bring her back
Till the Germans quit, and when the Allies win,
Till we nail the Union Jack on the Kaiser's chimney stack,
And we toast the Yukon daughters in Berlin.

Yukon soldiers went 8,000 miles to do battle for the Empire. They sent ten percent of their population to fight for King and country, and gave $20 a head to the Patriotic Fund—more than any other part of Canada. Martha never worked so hard as in London during the war years. Officially she was the keeper of the comforts for the troops, typing lists of wounded for the Red Cross, trundling to hospitals to visit Yukoners who had been injured. Martha Louise was the only woman from Dawson and many of the boys on leave found her small flat and made it home. Martha held them and fed them as they picked awkwardly at words to describe the terror of the trenches. Sometimes they showed Martha photographs of their "girl" or wife and children. Always they left feeling heard. They were Martha's boys and they called her the Mother of the Yukon. Her own sons and husband were fighting far away. News reached Martha of a nineteen-year-old Yukon boy who had caught a company of German cavalry rushing through his line—it was her own son Lyman. He was awarded the Military Cross for his bravery; Martha was there when King George V pinned the medal on the boy who was born in the cabin. Martha beamed.

When the war was over and the Canadian dead in their thousands buried, Martha Black and George came home. George entered federal politics as a Conservative candidate in the 1921 federal election and was elected to Parliament three times, finally becoming the Speaker of the House of Commons in 1930. Martha was again at the centre of affairs of state, playing hostess to visiting dignitaries to Canada, regaling them with her tales of derring-do during the gold rush. Then suddenly, she was shoved into the limelight.

George had a nervous breakdown and couldn't run for reelection; Martha Louise ran in his place. In a Liberal landslide, Martha Black won her seat as an independent. "I represent no political party," she said. "I represent the people of the Yukon." Martha became the second woman member of Parliament, joining Agnes McPhail, who had sat alone as the only woman for fifteen years. Martha Louise was seventy years old.

The celebration was short-lived. Only weeks after taking her seat, Lyman died in a car crash—he'd been driving from Kingston to visit his mother. Martha didn't miss a single day of work but she crumbled. "I am lonely. I feel bowed and broken for the first time in my life," she wrote in her diary. It was a season of losses. A few months later, forty-eight-year-old Warren died, Martha's first born. Then the funeral for her brother George, killed by tuberculosis. Martha's world was disappearing.

Duty braced her. Martha Louise sturdied herself in the service of her constituents. The former daughter of the American Revolution was now a member of the Imperial Order of the Daughters of the Empire. She stood for Canada's interests, voting against reciprocity with the United States, and lobbying for an international highway that would link Canada with Alaska.

Martha gave her seat back to George in the next election. In 1949 he retired and the Blacks headed back to Dawson. Martha Louise lived until she was ninety-one years old, among the friends and memories of her beloved Yukon. She died on October 31, 1957, an American-born Canadian nationalist who served King and country, and the interests of the Yukon.

American Immigration History in Canada

The act of migration is an adventure, whether journeying over an ocean, travelling from one continent to another, or, in the case of American immigrants to Canada, simply crossing the forty-ninth parallel. It was Martha Black's spirit of adventure that lured her away from Chicago's high-society life and onto the trail of the Klondike Gold Rush in 1898. While Martha invented a life for herself, most of the stampeders left Canada as abruptly as they came, never to return.

Nobody knows for sure how many Americans made similar journeys to Canada. Movement across the American and Canadian border was unregulated for centuries—in fact, the border itself kept moving as early French and English colonies swallowed each other up. As colonies on either side of the border grew into separate nations, common ancestry and similar cultures allowed for an easy back-and-forth. To make analysis even blurrier, Americans were never singled out in the Canadian census until 1991, when respondents had the opportunity to write in their place of origin if it wasn't among the options listed.

The United States of America has been one of the oldest and most enduring sources of Canadian immigrants. Over the years an estimated three million Americans emigrated here. The first were Yankee planters, who arrived in Nova Scotia in the mid-1700s, followed by the Loyalists, fleeing the American Revolution later in the century.

The largest wave of Americans to Canada occurred between 1895 and 1915. The frontier in rural America was coming to a close, ending an era in which good cheap land was available in seemingly unlimited quantities. At the same time, the railways were just opening up the Canadian West. American farmers poured into Canada, making up nearly as many of the western settlers as those from the British Isles. The effects of this migration can still be seen in the high American-born presence in Alberta and Saskatchewan and in the ratio of farmers among the American-born. Some argue it's also evident in political attitudes in these provinces, which differ dramatically from those in the rest of Canada.

The newly elected Liberal government reflected these changing economic conditions with its immigration law of 1896. Clifford Sifton, minister of the interior under Prime Minister Wilfrid Laurier, speaking to the Commons in 1902, explained that all government immigration policy was directed exclusively toward encouraging settlement of rural areas: "The test we have to apply is this," he said. "Does the person intending to come to Canada intend to become an agriculturalist? If he does, we encourage him to come and give him every assistance we can. But we give no encouragement whatever to persons who come to work for wages."

Despite various immigration restrictions over the years, the proximity of Canada to the United States has made for easy immigration and remigration. Between WW I and the 1970s, American citizens were less likely than other foreign nationals to become Canadian. But from 1902 to 1914, over 74,000 Americans became Canadians, making up over one-third of the total immigrants naturalized over this period. One-tenth of all American immigrants over the entire twentieth century have become Canadian citizens, making up seven percent of foreign-born nationals to do so.

Overcoming Obstacles

Martha Black escaped a suffocating life of social privilege to assert her independence in Canada. Many Americans have repeated that journey, though fleeing far worse circumstances. Refugee Americans include the Loyalists, fugitive black slaves, Vietnam war resisters and draft dodgers, and religious groups such as Mennonites and Hutterites. For them, Canada was a place of refuge and opportunity.

The Loyalists were American colonists on the side of the British during the American Revolution of 1775 to 1783, a war that won the Thirteen Colonies independence from Britain. An estimated 50,000 Loyalists fled to Canada, with the largest numbers coming between 1783 and 1784. The majority were farmers of varied ethnic backgrounds. Thirty thousand of them made the Maritime provinces home, often crowding out the native-born Acadians. The two main settlements were in the Saint John River valley and, temporarily, Shelburne, Nova Scotia. Another 2,000 settled in Quebec and 7,500 moved along the St. Lawrence, the Bay of Quinte, the Niagara Peninsula and the Detroit River. These were the Loyalists who made up the initial population base that led to the creation of the separate province of Upper Canada in 1791. Loyalists were quickly outnumbered by immigrants to come after, but they left an enduring influence. It is from the Loyalists that Canada inherited a certain conservatism, a preference for evolution rather than revolution in government matters, and an acceptance of a pluralistic and heterogeneous society.

The American Revolution Loyalists also brought 2,000 of their black slaves to a colony that hadn't known much slavery. Ironically, 3,500 free blacks who'd won their liberty by siding with Britain emigrated at the same time. They settled mostly in Nova Scotia and New Brunswick.

In 1793, Upper Canada became the only colony to legislate a gradual abolition of slavery. This precipitated a large wave of American blacks to come to Canada independently, using a network of secret routes known as the Underground Railway. At the time of the American Civil War, an estimated 30,000 black fugitives had made their way to Canada. When American slavery ended in 1865, many former slaves and black Canadians returned to the United States. The black population in Canada didn't grow substantially until the 1960s, when changes in immigration policy eliminated a bias against nonwhite immigrants.

American Mennonites, Amish and Hutterites were also lured to Canada. Often persecuted in the States, they came to Canada in search of freedom to exist in accordance with their pacifist beliefs and religious independence. The first Mennonite migration brought approximately 2,000 Swiss Mennonites from Pennsylvania to Upper Canada after the American Revolution. They bought land and settled on the Niagara Peninsula and in York and Waterloo counties. From 1825 to the mid-1870s about 750 Amish settled on Crown land in Waterloo County.

The biggest wave of Mennonites and Hutterites spilled onto the prairies between 1917 and 1918. In the patriotic fever of WW I, they'd been harassed for trying to avoid American conscription. Today, an estimated 200,000 Mennonites, Amish and Hutterites live in communal colonies scattered across Canada.

The Vietnam War sent another large wave of American immigrants spilling into Canada. Mostly young and male, the draft dodgers were pacifists, political dissidents and students who preferred learning to killing. In 1968 a *New York Times* article estimated that about 5,000 young Americans had taken refuge in Canada. It was generally believed that close to 30,000 draft-age Americans emigrated. Thirty years later, research suggests that between 60,000 and 140,000 Americans sought sanctuary in Canada.

The American-Canadian Legacy

One of the greatest legacies of American immigration is that of William Van Horne, who came to Canada as the general manager of the Canadian Pacific Railway in 1882. Van Horne organized the construction of the railway through the western mountains and prairies, completing the line between Winnipeg and Calgary by 1883 after years of delays. With Van Horne at the helm, the CPR developed a telegraph service and entered the express business. In 1891 he introduced the Empress line of steamships, a fleet of vessels that ran between Vancouver and Hong Kong, and later he founded the CP Hotels such as the Banff Springs in Alberta, the Chateau Frontenac in Quebec and the Chateau Laurier in Ottawa. As one of Canada's nation builders, Van Horne himself inevitably put down roots. "Building that railroad," as Van Horne said, "would have made a Canadian out of the German Emperor."

American settlers were renowned among leaders of western agrarian protest. One of the best-known American settlers in Canada since Confederation was Henry Wise Wood. Born into a prosperous farming family, he visited Alberta in 1904, heralded then as "the last best West," and purchased a wheat farm near Carstairs. In 1914 he became the director of the United Farmers of Alberta. From then until his death Wood was an influential political figure in Alberta, urging rural people to organize so as to counteract the power and the banks and capitalists.

C.D. Howe was another American settler who initially made his mark in agriculture. From 1915 to 1935, Howe became the leading grain-elevator builder of his time. His business crumpled in the Depression. In 1935 he entered Parliament as a Liberal and became a member of Mackenzie King's cabinet. Howe served as minister of transport and helped create Trans-Canada Airlines, later to become Air Canada. In 1940 he became minister of munitions and was responsible for Canada's war-production program, and four years later he took over the new department of reconstruction, restoring a largely free-market economic system. The next decade, he was instrumental in getting federal support for the trans-Canada pipeline.

Another American who became prominent in Canada was Walter Graves Penfield. In 1934 Penfield founded the Montreal Neurological Institute, where he introduced the "Montreal method," a new way of treating epilepsy through surgery. The institute quickly became an international centre of teaching, research and treatment for diseases of the nervous system, and remains so today.

And of course, Martha Black blossomed on Canadian soil. She developed an expertise on Yukon flora and gave extensive lectures about the beauty and history of the territory. She raised a family and succeeded in the milling business. In 1904 she married George Black and instantly became a loyal Canadian Conservative. When Black was appointed commissioner of the Yukon, Martha reigned as first lady. She followed her husband to England during WW I, receiving the Order of the British Empire for her aid to Yukon servicemen. She later became a fellow of the Royal Geographic Society for her work with Yukon flora. When George Black was unable to defend his Commons seat in 1935, Martha ran in his place. At the age of seventy, she campaigned the vast Yukon constituency, often by foot. As the second woman ever elected to Canadian Parliament, Martha Black became known and remembered well as the First Lady of the Yukon. America's loss and Canada's gain.

Sources

The Canadian Encyclopedia, World Edition, McClelland & Stewart, Toronto, 1998.

First Lady of the Yukon, Martha Black, directed by David Adkin. White Pine Pictures, Toronto, 1999.

The Fitzhenry & Whiteside Book of Canadian Facts & Dates, Jay Myers. Fitzhenry & Whiteside, Richmond Hill, 1991.

Klondike: The Last Great Gold Rush, 1896-1899, Pierre Berton. Penguin Books Canada/McClelland & Stewart, Toronto, 1972.

Klondike Women; True Tales of the 1897-98 Gold Rush, Melanie J. Mayer. Swallow Press/Ohio University Press, Ohio, 1989.

Martha Black: Gold Rush Pioneer, Carol Martin. Douglas & McIntyre, Vancouver, 1996.

My Ninety Years, Martha Louise Black. Alaska Northwest Publishing Company, Alaska, 1976.

My Seventy Years, Mrs. George Black, F.R.G.S., as told to Elizabeth Bailey Price. Thomas Nelson and Sons, London, 1938.

Only Farmers Need Apply, Harold Martin Troper. Griffin House, Toronto, 1972.

Women of the Klondike, Frances Backhouse. Whitecap Books, Toronto, 1995.

Morris Shumiatcher

Chasia and Judah (inset)

Chapter Eight
Something from Nothing: The Shumiatchers

Canada and the World in 1909

Two thousand coal miners strike in Alberta.

Governor General Lord Grey donates the Grey Cup to the best football team in Canada.

Gold is discovered in the Cochrane district of northern Ontario.

Naturalist Jack Miner begins the system of tagging birds at his bird sanctuary in Ontario.

The first flying exhibition for paying spectators in North America takes place at Scarborough Beach, near Toronto.

Adding machines, animal crackers, automobiles, BB guns, bottled beer, binoculars, snapshot cameras, comic strips, Crackerjack, electric flashlights, innerspring mattresses, linoleum, steam radiators, safety razors, wire window screens, Pepsi-Cola, teddy bears, tubed toothpaste and portable typewriters become available in the 1900s.

In the beginning there were Judah and Chasia Shumiatcher and then their eleven children, born amid the purges that regularly swooped down on Russian Jews. They were prisoners in their own country, the enemy within.

For a thousand years, Jews had been chased through Europe on the point end of Christian superstition, blamed for crop failures and plagues, prohibited from owning land. The last hundred years in Russia had been especially terrifying. Under the rule of Catherine the Great, Jews from conquered Poland had been absorbed reluctantly into the Russian Empire. They were refused settlement in ninety percent of Russia, including Moscow and St. Petersburg, and were forced into the "Pale of Settlement," twenty-five provinces along the western border. Five million Jews tried to live invisibly between the Baltic and Black seas. Generations of Shumiatchers had suffered the Czars' repressive edicts, been refused education, mobility, jobs; their children stolen from them and forced into twenty-five-year military service, often threatened with conversion. Jews had spent a century in the nervous isolation of their Russian shtetels, turning their proscribed energies into a vibrant, secretive culture.

The Shumiatcher children grew up in the warm breath and insular rhythms of Russian Judaism, and in the certainty of belonging to it. Their village life was embroidered with wonder and folklore and the dominating tenderness of their mother, Chasia. Around them, Jews scratched out work as tailors, innkeepers, cobblers, bakers, blacksmiths, dairymen, small shopkeepers, or simply *luftmentshen*—people who made a living out of air. Everyone was scraping together a few kopecks.

Judah was a fruit farmer, renting acreage just outside the city of Gomel, doing well for himself. Surrounded by unpredictable peasants who could turn violent on a rumour, the Shumiatchers lived parallel but apart, within their own laws. The *shochet*, or ritual slaughterer, provided whatever kosher meat there was, and sometimes doubled as *mohel,* circumcising baby boys on their eighth day after birth. In larger towns like Gomel, community councils maintained synagogues and paid rabbis and cantors. There was the *Khevra Kadisha*—holy society—which took care of burying the dead and maintaining cemeteries, and every village and town provided for its poor. Jews erected *hekdesh*—hospitals, infirmaries and orphanages—and *moshavei zkeinim,* old-age homes. In a country where eighty percent of the population was illiterate, almost all Jewish boys and most of the girls learned to read and write their own language. Half could read and write Russian.

The Shumiatchers might have spoken the local dialect, but at home their language was *mammeloshen,* the mother tongue, Yiddish. Hebrew was the language of prayer and study, reserved for the synagogue. Pious Jews like their father Judah read the Talmud, and both parents kept the dietary laws, as well as the Sabbath and holidays.

Of all the eleven Shumiatcher children, it was the second-born Morris who wanted to leave Russia most emphatically, and who prodded his father with heated arguments. In seventeen-year-old Morris's own lifetime, forty-five pogroms had swept across the Pale, wounding over four thousand Jews and killing ninety-three. The infamous massacre at Kishinev that had shocked the world in 1903 was followed by a pogrom right in Gomel itself. Half of the population of forty thousand was Jewish, but it hadn't stopped hundreds of Christian railway workers from rampaging through their neighbourhoods. A *New York Times* headline of September 24 read: "Russian Troops Aided the Slayers of Jews." Gomel Jews had fought back, encouraging other Jews across the Pale to do the same. But ten Jews had died and the whole community was blamed by the police for destroying their own homes. Who knew when the next attack would come? The only option was conversion to Christianity or emigration. Almost a million Jews were fleeing Russia.

Judah finally gave in to his son's exhortations. He had heard from his friend, the Gomel baker, who had left for Calgary, that Canada was giving free land to immigrants. Cramming into steerage, Judah and Morris headed across the sea, pulled by a thought that was almost too fantastic to entertain: a Jew owning land. On the other side, some Canadian politicians feared the arrival of hordes of Jews, but the west needed settlers and Prime Minister Wilfrid Laurier agreed to let them in.

A shudder went through the older, established Jewish community in Canada as boatloads of newcomers began arriving. Canadian Jews were better educated, integrated, quieter. The new arrivals came rushing in like a geyser, loud and obvious in their poverty, raggedy, religious Jews, foreign-looking. Everything they owned, they carried on their backs—pitiful bundles for the world to see. More Jews bunching up in Montreal or Toronto threatened the steady gains the Jewish community had worked so hard to win. Better that they should spread out and populate the west. Canadian Jews would eagerly help with money and settlement assistance, but they didn't want to see urban ghettoes.

Judah and Morris Shumiatcher stammered out their names in Halifax, trying to be understood. They couldn't speak any English, but they did know that their name started with S. The immigration official said, "Well, you know, when everyone's coming to a new country, they often change their name and Smith would be good for you." Morris didn't mind—maybe it was a good omen to start a new life with a new name. Anyway, he didn't want to hold up the immigration man, or lose his place in the line. Years later, Morris would tell his grandchildren this story a thousand times, and they would groan in boredom.

Judah and Morris Smith headed for the new western province of Alberta, and registered for their land. Through the CPR, they got a quarter section of land in Rumsey, about 100 miles outside of Calgary. Rumsey was Alberta's earliest Jewish farm colony, started in 1906 especially for the immigrants. Jewish farm settlements had been steadily dotting the prairies since 1882, when the worst pogroms had sent Jews fleeing into the world. Surprisingly, even though father and son had come in the cold of winter, they did well. Unlike most Russian Jews, the Smiths had farmed before, but their hunger for land came mostly from 2,000 years of exile. Still, it was the bustle of the city they yearned for, a place to make a better living and to be among a bigger Jewish community.

Calgary was booming, an agricultural centre not yet oil-rich, but growing on the wealth of cattle and wheat. It had been founded only thirty-six years before, by a dusty troop of North-West Mounted Police, chasing after American whisky runners. Colonel J.F. Macleod had pulled into a shady patch of trees at the crook of the Elbow and

Bow rivers and made a permanent camp. He called it Fort Calgary, a Gaelic word meaning running water.

By the new century, Calgary's population had exploded, from less than 5,000 in 1901 to 43,700 ten years later. A lot of the newcomers were from Ontario, but others had rushed in from all over Europe. Jews, too—600 by 1911. The first Jewish congregation had been pieced together five years earlier, the founding *minyan*—the ten men required for a congregation—made up of two Calgarians, two Edmontonians, five commercial travellers, and a farmer from Lacombe who came to Calgary to be with his own people during the High Holidays.

Judah made an immediate impact. He had carried with him, all the way from Russia, a Torah scroll. It was the first of its kind in the city. He took over as *shamas*, a sextant, and helped to look after the new synagogue, called Beth Jacob. In 1912, the Hebrew Free School opened and Judah became one of its first instructors, teaching Hebrew.

The rest of the family hurried to Calgary in 1911, eleven more Shumiatchers, the youngest one only three. They settled in a big home on Fourth Avenue and took in boarders to make extra money—there were at least sixteen people for dinner every night. The children under twelve went to school and lost their accents; the children over twelve went to work and kept theirs. Morris found his first Calgary job making wood mouldings at the A.B. Cushings sawmill, and for a time was the family's main breadwinner. But he had a secret dream of becoming an actor.

The Smiths mastered English, many of them at night school, and quickly adjusted to the wide-open ways of a cowboy town. Calgary's cowboy identity was just taking shape in the national imagination, helped by the first Calgary Stampede in 1912. An American trick roper, Guy Weadick, had figured that the emerging town was a prime location for a big rodeo. Originally billed as "The Greatest Outdoor Show on Earth," the event was a great success from the beginning. At the 1912 Stampede, the Duke and Duchess of Connaught and their daughter, Princess Patricia, officiated, and 2,000 natives in full dress thrilled a crowd of 14,000 spectators. Here was the bareback bronc riding, bull riding, steer wrestling and calf roping that would define a way of life to the world. No one suspected that the Smith family fortunes would be so tightly wound around the Stampede. Least of all Morris.

He'd pursued his dream of becoming an actor, going down to Hollywood in 1913. He stayed about a year and half, almost starving on the puny cheques he got for walk-on roles. He came back to Calgary and joined the army. That was no life, either, and Morris got out in 1919. He pondered his options—there were a lot of service jobs, and the beef and wheat industries; maybe what Calgary needed was some kind of secondary industry, some manufacturing. He went to the library and read up on business opportunities. When he stumbled on some photographs of hats, inspiration struck. Morris needed a $300 loan to convert a cleaning and blocking establishment called Calgary Hat Works, into a hat manufacturer and retailer. The bank refused him the money because he had no collateral, and suggested that Morris's brother Harry could co-sign a loan. Harry had a successful business only a few blocks down the street selling newspapers and magazines: Harry's News; later, another brother would start Billy's News. Morris was a bit indignant at first—if his signature wasn't good enough, then forget it. But the next day he was back. He'd reconsidered and, of course, Harry signed for him and he had the $300. By 1920 Smithbilt Hats was a bona fide company and Morris was ordering bolts of felt and manufacturing hats from beginning to end. Two years later, Judah Smith died. It was left to Chasia to hold her brood together.

She reigned over the big house on Fourth Avenue, the heart of her family. It was such a large, sprawling bunch, four boys and seven girls, that their home became a gathering place for any Jew wandering into town. And the girls were a magnet for crowds of prospective husbands. After Annie married in 1917, it was inevitable that the others would follow. The house contracted as Eva, Bella, Sarah, Fannie, Esther and Bessie each left on the arm of their grooms. Four of the girls became accomplished musicians, while Esther became a well-known Yiddish poet, touring the world with her husband, writer Peretz Hirshbein. Many of the sisters moved to New York City, the real centre for Jewish culture in North America, but they always came back, at least to visit.

It didn't take long for the house to swell up again with grandchildren, twenty-three of them, crowding into the Calgary home for regular family get-togethers: Hannukah, Yom Kippur, Rosh Hashanah. Grandmother Chasia held everyone close, making sure that the children had what they wanted, and if not, why not? Often she took the bus to her grandchildren's homes, appearing early in the morning with porridge. In the world of want that she had come from, Chasia made it her life's work to provide for everyone.

Her children and grandchildren didn't keep kosher or the Sabbath as Chasia did, but they were committed to Judaism. They started Yiddish day schools and became leaders in other Jewish organizations, embracing their parents' values and the essential importance of family celebrating life together. The Smiths prodded and elbowed each other forward, telling one another how smart they were, how handsome, how talented. It left a good feeling, a worthiness that stretched through four generations.

One of the things the Smiths loved to do together was drive up to the mountains, especially when the New York family came to visit every summer. Their trips to Banff consisted of a long cavalcade, with children crowded into backseats. Chasia prepared picnics with extraordinary amounts of roast chicken, vegetables and baked goods. The grandchildren would recall the ritual fondly.

"Have another piece of chicken," Chasia would plead.

"No, but thank you. It was really delicious," one of the children would reply.

"If it's so delicious, why don't you have another piece of chicken?"

"But I've had enough chicken."

"You don't like the chicken?"

"I'll have another piece of chicken."

The first generation of Smiths had seized every opportunity Calgary had to offer. The eldest son, Abe, became a lawyer, and Billy and Harry operated their news and tobacco stores. Morris continued running his Smithbilt Hat factory and its retail stores in Alberta, Saskatchewan and British Columbia all through the hard hurt of the Depression and World War II, producing and selling mostly fedoras. Then he switched to a western style when the cowboy hat became more and more popular.

After the war, Morris noticed that people were looking for lighter-coloured hats. He decided to take a chance on a white one, and became the first hat maker to produce a pure white cowboy hat. People grabbed them up. The Calgary Stampede Board had been encouraging Calgarians to wear cowboy hats during the Stampede and they came to Morris and talked about it. He ordered enough white felt to make eighteen hats. Calgary rancher and oilman Bill Herron bought four for his family to wear in the Stampede parade, the rest sold out in a single afternoon. The following year Smithbilt made 240 white cowboy hats for the Stampede, which sold just as fast as the year before. White hats and the Calgary Stampede were becoming synonymous.

Morris's luck got even better. Smithbilt cowboy hats went national at the Grey Cup game in Toronto. The Grey Cup trophy had been part of Canadian sports since 1909, but in 1948, the Calgary Stampeders were competing for their first championship against Ottawa. Morris's son Judah and his nephew Maurice Paperny, were at university in Toronto and Montreal, and he sent them some hats in case there might be a local demand for them when the western team rolled into town. The boys took out a peddler's licence and began hawking hats in downtown Toronto, at the corner of Yonge and King streets. It was days before the game, and they didn't sell more than half a dozen hats. But that was all about to change.

Calgary fans were on their way to Toronto, bringing the Stampede with them—six palomino and pinto horses, a chuckwagon and a piano were hauled on freight cars. The Stampeders partied all the way east and hit Toronto with more impact than a keg of beer on the side of the head.

"Many people say the Grey Cup never amounted to much until a couple of train-loads of uninhibited Albertans arrived in 1948 to show staid old Toronto how the thing should be run," wrote Tony Allan in his book *Grey Cup or Bust*. "They certainly boosted the sales of white Stetsons, if nothing else."

Two hundred yelping Calgarians got off their seventeen-car "Stampeder Special" at Toronto's Union Station and broke into a spontaneous square dance, hurling each other across the station floor to the accompaniment of accordion music. Someone twirled a lasso, roping in locals. Women in red blouses and men in chaps and spurs were all wearing their white Smithbilt hats.

The show moved outside and held up traffic for ten minutes as the Calgarians crossed the street to the Royal York Hotel. A horse and rider showed up in the hotel lobby. Calgary Alderman Don McKay dared Toronto Mayor Hiram McCallum to ride a horse down Bay Street the morning of the game. The next day, chefs in Smithbilt cowboy hats served up a flapjack breakfast on the steps of

Toronto's City Hall. It was a week of all-out, western-style partying. Toronto had never raised its eyebrows so high.

Judah and Maurice, managed to deposit several hats in the United Cigar Stores in both the Royal York Hotel and the King Edward Hotel in Toronto. Smithbilts were selling at a furious pace as the whole country woke up to the Grey Cup.

The Calgary team was the underdog. Using game film was illegal back then, but Calgary coach Les Lear somehow got hold of Ottawa's film and played it for his team. When the Stampeders got on the field with their red-and-white striped sweaters and helmets, Ottawa grabbed a one-nothing lead in the first quarter. Then Calgary ran circles around them. The winning touchdown belonged to the Stampeders. The score: twelve to seven.

As the final whistle blew, Calgary fans rose out of their seats and surged onto the field. Judah and his cousin Maurice were part of the crowd that tore down the goalposts and carried them out of the stadium. They had to break the window of a streetcar to hoist the goal posts in, then they marched them into the Royal York Hotel. As drinks were passed they hollered out the Calgary chant:

We're here for this one reason,
For an undefeated season
And the Grey Cup win today
Yieeayeah, yippee cayeah

In the festivities, someone found a hand saw and started slicing off bits of the posts to sell as souvenirs for

$1 a piece. A guitar-playing duo jumped up on a table and began belting out cowboy songs, while wobbly voices joined in. In the background, hotel staff were sprinting through the lobby, carrying off furniture for safe-keeping.

The next day, the team, their fans and animals left Toronto, by some reports $100,000 richer for having bet $40,000 at eight-to-five odds against their heroes. The group partied all the way back to Calgary and arrived to a civic welcome, while the Smith boys stayed behind, doing a roaring sidewalk and department store trade. Everybody wanted their hats: Eaton's, Hudson's Bay and the menswear stores.

Morris Smith had conquered the country. White Smithbuilt cowboy hats became as much a part of the Grey Cup as Stampede chuckwagons—a national reminder of who we are and how the west was built.

The next year Calgary city Alderman Don McKay became mayor, and handed out the white cowboy hat to every visiting dignitary. By the time he left office in 1959, the hat that Smith built had become an internationally recognized sign of western hospitality. In fact, when Prince Philip came through town for a third time and was presented with a white hat, he said, "Oh, not another one."

It must have made Chasia proud. She lived to the age of eighty-eight, dying in 1955, surrounded by her eleven children. The last glimpse of Russia and of Orthodox ways faded with her. The family grieved for a very long time.

Three years later, Morris died and Judah became the proprietor of Smithbilt. Morris died a Shumiatcher, rather than a Smith, after a lifetime of changing his name back and forth. He'd first decided to go back to Shumiatcher when many of his siblings had started to. Friends told him he was crazy; they all knew him as Smith and the name was associated with the famous Smithbilt Hats. He agreed, and changed his name back to Smith. A few years later he was calling himself Morris Shumiatcher again.

For the next generation of Shumiatchers and Smiths, the greatest honour came in 1988, when Calgary hosted the Winter Olympics. Smithbilt hats were worn by the Canadian athletes at the opening ceremonies, and nobody in the family will ever forget the beauty of that moment. The Canadian team, led by figure skater Brian Orser and Chef de Mission Kean Grenier, entered the McMahon Stadium last, to a standing ovation from the international audience. They were dressed in long red coats with white, western-style leather fringes falling from their shoulders and on their heads, white Smithbilt hats.

Today, the walls of the Smithbilt factory are hung with pictures of celebrities smiling under those famous white cowboy hats. One of them is Mikhail Gorbachev, the former president of the Soviet Union, whose ancestors had probably forced Jews like the Shumiatchers out of Russia. But Canada had offered them a safe refuge from Russian pogroms and marginalization, and from the later horror of invading Nazis, who almost extinguished Jewish life in Russia, Poland and across Europe.

As the fourth and fifth generation of Canadian Shumiatchers are called upon to read from the Torah, as they make their mark in law, music, film, literature, medicine and architecture, their family ties and Jewish faith keep them firmly attached to the dreams of their ancestors. For behind each of them stands the indomitable spirit and lasting legacy of Judah, Chasia, Morris and the ten other original Shumiatchers who arrived empty-handed and created a national symbol that has reached into the world. It was something from nothing, and now it belongs to us all.

Jewish Immigration History in Canada

Unlike most immigrants to Canada, Jews didn't come from a single homeland, nor were they the majority culture in the places they emigrated from. Jews were dispersed at the time of the ancient Roman Empire and lived sometimes for many centuries as minorities in the Middle East, North Africa and Europe.

When the Shumiatchers arrived in Alberta in 1909, Russian Jews had been making their way to Canada for almost thirty years. By the end of the nineteenth century, eighty percent of the world's ten million Jews lived in the Russian, Austro-Hungarian and German empires. When horrific pogroms were initiated and violent mobs attacked Jewish neighbourhoods, Russian Jews fled into the wider world for refuge, including Canada. But the New World wasn't so new—Jews had been arriving in Canada for a century and a half. They helped finance the very founding of this nation and predated British colonization. It was an act of courage, even then.

Under the first French colonists, non-Catholics were forbidden to settle in New France. Some Jews manoeuvred around the law by converting to Catholicism or, like the Marranos, the Jewish refugees from the Spanish Inquisition, by pretending to convert while secretly practising their religion. In one of the most striking historical ironies of Canada, it was a Jewish family from Bordeaux, France, who, barred from living in the colony themselves, provided much of the goods and finances that kept New France alive.

In 1748, the Gradis family became partners in a chartered company, La Société du Canada. Putting up all the capital to supply goods to New France, and sharing only half the profits, the Gradises played a pivotal role in sustaining the colony before it was conquered by the British. They had a fleet of ships that went back and forth to France, providing food, supplies and munitions that kept the settlers armed and fed during their fight to defend the colony.

But Jewish political allegiances were as varied as anyone else's. While the Gradis family supported the French, Alexander Shomberg was a commander in the invading British navy. Of course, Schomberg's Jewishness had to be kept secret—only Christians were allowed to serve in the British navy. Schomberg's frigate, *Diana*, took part in the attack on Quebec that led to the battle on the Plains of Abraham, where the French colony fell to British control.

The British proved far more tolerant of Jews than the French. Though they didn't permit Jews citizenship in England, under a special act of Parliament in 1740, they allowed Jews to be naturalized in the colonies. By 1752, about thirty Jewish settlers were established in Halifax, many of them of German background who had come up from the American colonies. One of them, Isaac Levy, was the first person to try to exploit the Cape Breton coalfields. Abraham Hart founded the potash industry, while his brother Samuel became a leading merchant and was elected to the Nova Scotia assembly in 1793. Samuel Hart was the first Jew in the British Empire to hold a seat in a legislature.

The first significant wave of Jewish immigrants to Canada arrived with General Jeffery Amherst in 1760. Most of these Jewish settlers emigrated from the United States and settled in urban centres, the majority in Montreal. It was here, in 1768, that the Jewish community established Canada's first synagogue, Shearith Israel. By the late eighteenth century, Jews had also settled in Quebec City and other parts of Lower Canada. The Hart family was prominent in the area of Trois-Rivières; Ezekiel Hart was elected to the legislature of Lower Canada in 1807 but was denied his seat on the basis of his religion.

Most of the Jewish immigrants in this first wave were middle class and well educated, contributing to the economic growth of the country through trade. By Confederation, there were 1,115 Jews in Canada, the majority in Montreal and Toronto. But smaller groups spread across the country. A community of over one hundred settled in British Columbia when it joined Confederation. British Columbia's first delegation to the House of Commons included Henry Nathan, the first Jewish-Canadian MP.

Almost 15,000 Jewish immigrants came to Canada in the last half of the nineteenth century, mostly from Europe. When the Shumiatcher family crossed the sea in 1909, they were part of a group of 120,000 Jews that came from Eastern Europe between 1900 and 1920. By the time the outbreak of WW I curbed immigration, there were over 100,000 Jews in Canada. They toiled as retailers and wholesalers, working their way up to established businesses through the humble beginnings of peddling. Jews offered their labour to the urban sweatshops of the new ready-to-wear clothing industry, while Jewish merchants spread out to small towns, adding synagogues to the places of worship found in rural Canada. Sixty thousand more Jews came between 1920 and 1940, and another 135,000 arrived between WW II and the 1980s.

The Canadian Jewish population today is estimated at 356,000, the fifth-largest Jewish community in the world, behind the United States, Israel, the former USSR and France. Jewish immigration to Canada continues: 30,000 Jews entered Canada from 1981 to 1991. Today the largest Jewish population in Canada—about 162,000—is in Toronto.

Overcoming Obstacles

Between 1850 and 1914 Jewish immigrants faced few difficulties in gaining admission. But restrictions tightened after World War I and throughout the Depression years, at the very time upheavals in Europe made Jews more desperate than ever to leave, especially from Russia, Poland, Austria-Hungary, Romania and the Baltic states. Virulent anti-Semitism drove many Jews from their homeland, while thousands who stayed were massacred or victimized by disease and starvation.

Even with the rise of Hitler and the Nazi regime in the mid 1930s, refuge for Jewish immigrants was shamefully hard to find. Traditional countries of immigration, including Canada, imposed restrictions against Jews, leaving them at the mercy of their homeland. Condemned Jews in Auschwitz had a poignant vision of what this country represented. They named one of the barracks "Canada"—a place where food, clothes and confiscated belongings were stored. It was regarded as a place of luxury and salvation. But the real Canada was closed off to Jews between 1933 and 1945.

In 1939, Canadian Jews could only watch with helplessness and horror as the *St. Louis*, a ship full of more than 900 Jewish refugees, sailed from port to port in the United States and Latin America in desperate search of refuge. Canadian Prime Minister William Lyon Mackenzie King responded to the urgent pleas of the passengers by saying it was not a Canadian problem. With that, the Jews of the *St. Louis* headed back to Europe, many of them to their death. Between 1939 and 1945, Canada accepted a total of only 500 refugees, proportionately fewer Jews than any Western country. At the same time, 17,000 Jewish Canadians responded to the call to arms in WW II and served in the armed forces.

Anti-Semitism was spreading across Canada. The Social Credit Party, the Orange Order and the Native Sons of Canada fanned anti-Jewish feeling. Through the 1920s and 1930s, many industries didn't hire Jews, and universities and professional schools discriminated against them. Jewish doctors couldn't get hospital appointments or operating privileges. There were no Jewish judges, and Jewish lawyers were excluded from most firms. Signs warning "No Jews or Dogs Allowed" or "Christians Only!" were hung outside Halifax golf courses, hotels in the Laurentians, cottage areas of Ontario, the lake country of Manitoba and the vacation lands of B.C.

The Jewish-Canadian Legacy

Despite the obstacles some Jewish immigrants faced in finding a new homeland and starting over in Canada, Jewish society and culture have thrived and flourished here. The synagogue has long been the centre of the community's social and philanthropic work. In fact, the building of synagogues is often used as a benchmark of a community's success and progress in putting down roots. Canada's first synagogue, Shearith Israel, was established in Montreal in 1768. Toronto's first synagogue, later called the Holy Blossom Temple, was built in 1856.

There are several forms of religious expression in Jewish culture and many degrees of orthodoxy. Judaism is the ancient Jewish religious tradition that goes back thousands of years and predates Christianity. Modern forms of Jewish religious expression include the more secular Yiddish culture and Zionism, which helped to create the modern state of Israel.

Since the biblical origins of the Jews, and throughout their history of migration and resettlement, religion has been the main cohesive force in protecting and perpetuating Jewish identity. Most Jewish children in Canada attend public schools, but almost every Jewish community provides facilities for Yiddish and Jewish education. In urban areas such as Toronto, Montreal, Vancouver and Winnipeg, there are numerous Jewish day schools, some of which are partially funded by provincial governments. A significant number of Jewish children now attend these day schools. Some Canadian universities have developed programs of Judaic studies.

Jewish immigrants also brought a tradition of establishing a communal body to look after their own social welfare needs. The first Jewish social welfare body in Canada was the Young Men's Hebrew Benevolent Society, founded in Montreal in 1863 to help Jewish immigrants (in recognition of financial support, the name was changed to the Baron de Hirsch Institute in 1900). Montreal and Toronto, with large populations, developed a wide range of communal organizations: hospitals, social work agencies, homes for the aged, libraries and more. There was a gradual movement toward the formation of organizations to coordinate fundraising in local communities. Immigrant Jews also founded *landsmenschaften*, literally organizations of people from the same place. *Landsmenschaften* would sometimes sponsor synagogues, but they were primarily organizations in which immigrants helped each other and which could reply, as a group, to appeals for help from those left behind.

Today, Jews are among the most philanthropic contributors to Canadian society, especially in the arts, and play prominent roles in the political and cultural spheres of Canadian life. One of the first Jews to enter Canadian politics was Ezekiel Hart, who was elected to the legislature of Lower Canada in 1807. Hart could not take his seat, however, because the law of the time demanded that an oath of the Christian faith be taken. This obstacle was removed in 1832, at the same time that Jews were granted the same civil and political rights as other Canadians. It was this kind of progressive and humanistic legislation, twenty-five years before similar legislation was passed in

Britain, that helped shape Canada into a truly sovereign and multicultural nation.

Since then, Canadian Jews have been represented in all Canadian political parties: Allan Grossman, the first Jew appointed to the cabinet of a provincial government (Progressive Conservative); his son, the late Larry Grossman, the first Jew to be elected leader of an Ontario provincial party, the Progressive Conservative Party; Dave Barrett, the first Jew ever to be elected premier of a province (British Columbia); Stephen Lewis, the first Jewish leader of the Ontario New Democratic Party; his father, David Lewis, former leader of the national New Democratic Party. Herb Gray was the first Jewish cabinet minister, David Croll the first Jewish senator.

Jews have made deep and profound contributions to Canadian literature and art, including: Leonard Cohen, Garth Drabinsky, Ed Mirvish, A.M. Klein, Irving Layton, Mordecai Richler, Lorne Greene, John Hirsch, Johnny Wayne and Frank Shuster, Barbara Frum, Peter C. Newman, the Bronfman family, the Reichmann family and Sam Steinberg.

The Shumiatcher family, with roots in Canada going back to the beginning of the century, is truly representative of the Jewish immigrant experience, and of the Jewish legacy of active participation in Canadian society. Second- and third-generation Shumiatchers have become poets, writers, filmmakers, architects, lawyers, businessmen, judges and educators. Looking back, Maurice Paperny, grandson of Judah and Chasia Shumiatcher, recognizes the long road his family has journeyed over. "I think Judah and Chasia would have been very proud of their grandchildren," he says. "And even prouder of their great-grandchildren, because the seeds have truly scattered."

Sources

A Coat of Many Colours: Two Centuries of Jewish Life in Canada, Irving Abella. Lester & Orpen Dennys, Toronto, 1990.

The Fitzhenry & Whiteside Book of Canadian Facts & Dates, Jay Myers. Fitzhenry & Whiteside, Richmond Hill, 1991.

History of Jews in Canada, Benjamin G. Sack. Harvest House, Montreal, 1965.

It's How You Play the Game: The Inside Story of the Calgary Olympics, Frank W. King. The Writer's Group, Calgary, 1991.

The Jewish Community in Canada, Stuart E. Rosenberg. McClelland & Stewart, Toronto, 1971.

Jews: An Account of their Experience in Canada, Erna Paris. Macmillan, Toronto, 1980.

Journey into Our Heritage, Harry Gutkin. Lester & Orpen Dennys, Toronto, 1980.

Legends of Autumn: The Glory Years of Canadian Football, Denny Boyd and Brian Scrivner. Douglas & McIntyre, Vancouver, 1997.

None Is Too Many: Canada and the Jews of Europe, 1933-1948, Irving Abella and Harold Troper. Lester & Orpen Dennys, Toronto, 1982.

Pogroms: Anti-Jewish Violence in Modern Russian History, John D. Klier and Shlomo Lambroza, editors. Cambridge University Press, Cambridge, 1992.

"The Shumiatcher Saga," by Brian Brennan, *Calgary Herald*, March 8–10, 1997.

Something from Nothing, directed by David Paperny. White Pine Pictures, 1998.

Striking Roots: Reflections on Five Decades of Jewish Life, Aron Horowitz. Mosaic Press, Oakville, 1979.

Taking Root: The Origins of the Canadian Jewish Community, Gerald Tulchinsky. Lester Publishing, Toronto, 1992.

Bagga Singh

Chapter Nine
Passage from India: Bagga Singh

Canada and the World in 1913

Alys Bryant is the first woman in Canada to make a solo plane flight, from a Vancouver racetrack.

The Ontario Department of Instruction bans the use of French in Ontario schools past Grade One.

The Canadian Northern railway completes a tunnel under Mount Royal in Montreal.

The Bank of New Brunswick merges with the Bank of Nova Scotia.

The number of immigrants to Canada reaches an all-time record: 400,870.

Brillo pads, Corn Flakes, packaged cheese, crossword puzzles, electric trains, Jell-O, margarine, packaged mayonnaise, paper towels, road maps, outboard motors, sneakers, Tinkertoys, electric toasters and vacuum cleaners, became widely available in the 1910s.

In the spring of 1914, Vancouver braced itself for the arrival of a boatload of Punjabis. For weeks, newspaper headlines shrieked with dire warnings, as if the Mogul hordes themselves were descending. Antagonism had been sharpening against South Asians for a decade. Bagga Singh had felt its point end as he'd made his way into British Columbia the year before. He'd been lured away from his wife and children in their village of Saraba in northern India by stories of opportunity. But a ban on

Asian immigration had forced him to sneak into the country from California.

A year later, twenty-four-year-old Bagga and the entire Sikh community twitched in anticipation, bending toward the Pacific for the approach of hope. A ship called the *Komagata Maru* was steaming across the world to challenge Canadian immigration law. Only a decade before, one of the local newspapers had trumpeted another ship of South Asians as the first Sikhs came ashore at Vancouver. "Turbaned Men Excite Interest: Awe-inspiring Men from India Held the Crowds" was how they announced the event.

In 1902, thousands of delegates from across the Empire had been invited to the coronation of Edward VII, and Sikhs came trooping through Canada on their way to England. Vancouverites crowded the streets for a peek at the Punjabis, flushed with imperial pride as they watched the troops that had defended the Empire two years before in the siege of Peking. The Sikhs performed drills, were inspected by Governor General Minto in Ottawa, and were then presented with the Cross of India by the King in England. The Sikhs returned home with stories of Canadian wealth and welcome that inched across the impoverished Punjab. Over the next ten years, 5,000 Sikhs headed for Canada. One was Bagga Singh, who left his wife and two daughters for the riches of the Dominion.

Bagga didn't find welcome among the once-adoring Anglo-Saxons. Vancouver was hostile and market forces were his single ally. Cheap labour was in short supply as Chinese immigrants headed east, out of the way of B.C.'s stinging racism. Sikhs replaced them on the fruit farms and in the forest industry. Bagga found a job in a sawmill and a home in a bunkhouse, cramming into a spartan slapped-up shack. It was grim; 100 Sikh workers lived together, with a single cook to make the meals. Every evening workers left the mill carrying a block of wood for the huge kitchen stove. Every evening Bagga's clothes were covered in sawdust and the resiny scent of fresh lumber. It was a smell that would hover over the Sikh community for two generations.

Bagga worked with the biggest trees in Canada, feeding cedar, balsam and Douglas firs into the mills, sawing wood for local settlements and the growing prairie towns. British Columbia was producing sixty percent of Canada's sawn lumber, and Bagga Singh was helping to house a nation, though his own homes were little more than ghettos as he moved from job to job.

Sikhs crowded into lodging houses all over B.C. As many as ten men shared a single room for cooking, eating and sleeping, saving money to send back home. Canadians hated it. Edwardian sensibilities curdled at the raw living conditions of the foreigners, perhaps a little envious of the economic advantages of Sikh frugality. European Canadians called them degraded, uncivilized and worse, refusing to serve them in stores and restaurants or allow them into certain neighbourhoods. Bagga had to learn to manoeuvre through the hard-heartedness, to move carefully, to plan his route. He had to learn to keep his face blank, his eyes unseeing. Without a wife and family to steer him into the larger world of schools and neighbours, he burrowed into his own.

The Sikh community was a bachelor society—only nine Sikh women were allowed into Canada between 1904 and 1920. Bagga pooled his money for rent, fuel, food, helping out in the common kitchen and sharing a basic meal of chapatis—unleavened bread—lentils and curry. Every morning after bathing, Bagga would recite passages from the *Guru Granth Sahib*—the holy book. Often he attended *gurdwara*—temple—bowing his head to the ground and making an offering. There everyone would then recite the a*rdas*, the Sikh prayers and the final proclamation, "Raj Karega Khalsa"—the Khalsa shall rule.

It was a bare-bones communal life, monklike, with its own small epiphanies and friendships and an unflagging sense of duty to provide for others. Bagga made about $9 a week and paid about $2 for room and board, while sending the rest back home. Low living costs were a cushion against hard times and allowed Sikhs to support their own sick or jobless in Canada. Cooking duties were often delegated to unemployed friends. When 1,000 Indians were out of work in the Depression of 1907, even the government had to admit that they were well provided for privately. But two years later, British Columbia took away their right to vote. Without the franchise, men like Bagga Singh couldn't enter professions, get government contracts or vote federally. They were forbidden jobs in public works or with forestry companies cutting on Crown land. Federal politicians like Labour Minister Mackenzie King claimed that "the Hindu is not suited to the climate of this country."

It was galling to be called a Hindu. Technically, Bagga was an Indian, but he was a member of a 400-year-old religion that had rejected Hindu authority. Sikhism was a profound reform movement similar to the Protestant reformation. It had rebelled against the Hindu caste system and the corruption of political tyranny. Sikhs refused the Indian aesthetic tradition of withdrawal from the world and what they saw as the hollow pretensions of ritual. Founder Guru Nanak and his nine successors had each carved out a deeper Sikh spiritual and social distinctiveness. Women were considered equals. Purdah, the seclusion of women, and the horrific Hindu practice of suttee, the forced burning of widows on their husbands' funeral pyres, were abolished. The practice of *langar,* community kitchen, brought rich and poor to eat and worship together. It was a religion of hope and justice, especially for the excluded.

Sikh history was strewn with heroic men and women, and martyrs who had been sawn in half, beheaded, boiled in oil by their Hindu and Muslim rivals. The tenth and last guru had created the Khalsa (pure), a devout society where initiated men took the last name Singh (lion) and women, the name Kaur (princess). Men of the Khalsa observed five tenets: to keep their beards and hair uncut and to wear a comb, a steel bracelet, soldier's breeches and a dagger. Bagga Singh was emphatically not a Hindu. It didn't matter.

"Canada is best left in the hands of the Anglo-Saxon race....[I]t shall remain white and our doors shall be closed to the Asians," said MP Herbert Stevens, the leader of the Asiatic Exclusion League. Stevens had lit the match that had set off a powder keg of hate. White Canadian mobs had rampaged against "Asiatic" immigrants in 1907, and then again in 1913. A cabinet minister was sent to negotiate limiting immigration with the Japanese government, and Mackenzie King went to London to appeal to the colonial undersecretary, Winston Churchill, for a ban on Sikhs. Immigration policies toughened. The government demanded Punjabis have $200 in their possession upon arrival, while European immigrants needed only $25. Then it demanded that South Asians come by continuous journey from India, an impossibility because steamship companies were instructed by the government not to provide the service. While not banning Indian immigration outright, the Law of Direct Passage had the same effect.

The *Komagata Maru* was about to challenge the law by adhering to it exactly. A feisty Sikh businessman in Hong Kong had hired a ship to carry Sikhs on a direct passage from India. With a hefty down payment and a promise to pay the balance when the freighter reached Vancouver, Gurdit Singh went about selling tickets to hopeful Sikhs. Most left without the required $200 entry money, but Gurdit was certain he could raise the funds in the Vancouver Sikh community and convince Canadian immigration authorities to let the ship in. If it worked, a fleet of his freighters could carry passengers and cargo monthly, maybe weekly, after that.

On May 21, after seven dreary weeks at sea, the *Komagata Maru* arrived at the Victoria quarantine station with 376 passengers on board, including two women and three children. Two days later it pulled into Vancouver and anchored in Burrard Inlet. The Canadian government immediately placed an armed guard in a launch that circled the ship day and night. The passengers were virtual prisoners and not allowed to make contacts with the Vancouver Sikh community. Gurdit Singh's position was simple: by virtue of being British subjects, the passengers had the right to visit any part of the British empire. The Canadian government firmly disagreed.

Bagga and his Sikh countrymen were British citizens, if a little unwillingly. For over 400 years they had defended their independence, standing up to the brutal incursions of the Mogul empire and the Hindus. They were finally trampled by the British in 1846. A year later, the Sikhs saved their conquerors.

England had not endeared itself to its Indian sepoys, or soldiers. Resentments festered over poor pay and imperial disregard. The sepoys finally mutinied over what they considered a religious blasphemy—the cartridges for their new Enfield rifles had been greased with cow and pig fat, offending both Hindus and Muslims. When sepoys murdered their British officers at Meerut and each group began marching toward their dream of taking over India, England looked for allies. Sikhs had never forgotten how the Hindu troops had betrayed them to the British conquerors. Nor, after years of fighting Moguls, did they want to live under Muslim rule. They joined the British forces marching toward Delhi and fought ferociously. After that, the British enlisted them into the British Army and Sikhs served faithfully at posts all through the empire. Now they were arguing to get into Canada.

The Sikhs on board the *Komagata Maru* had persuaded a crewman to take a note to the *gurdwara* secretary, asking for help. News spread throughout the Sikh community, infuriating Bagga Singh; with fourteen men, he helped organize the Shore Committee and mounted a court challenge. They found a lawyer to defend the passengers and the committee offered to make bail while the case dragged on, and to pay the $22,000 charter debt. The ship's owners conspired with the immigration officials, promising that they'd make sure the debt wasn't paid.

Prime Minister Robert Borden wanted to avert an international incident and hurried to get rid of the *Komagata Maru*. Ninety passengers were falsely declared to have trachoma, an infectious eye disease, and were barred from entering Canada. To further expedite deportation, Borden and his cabinet decided that the fate of all the passengers would rest on a single test case. Under Canadian law, all 356 passengers had the right to submit individual applications to the Immigration Board of Inquiry, and if they were rejected, each applicant could file a writ of habeas corpus, charging he was being illegally detained. This was the kind of stalling tactic that would build up the negative publicity the government wanted to avoid. The Sikhs refused.

On June 1, Bagga Singh and the Shore Committee organized a protest meeting in Vancouver's Dominion Hall. Six hundred Indians attended, along with twenty white supporters and a few reporters. The committee repeated its plea like a prayer from the Guru Granth Sahib—they needed hard cash, enough to keep the ship in Vancouver while its status was negotiated. The crowd swelled up with purpose; people who had been made small and invisible hurried to help. The hall was full of men who had never banked, who carried savings in their pockets or turbans. Money spilled out: a pile of $5, $10 and even $100 bills rose on a table in front of the speakers. The largest contribution was $2,000. At the end of the meeting, $5,000 in cash lay on the table. By June 10, Bagga Singh and the others on the Shore Committee had collected over $20,000, which went to the unpaid balance for the charter of the ship. Altogether the committee eventually raised an astronomical $70,000.

Weeks dragged by and conditions on the *Komagata Maru* deteriorated. Passengers became sick and one died. Garbage was piling up and immigration officials refused to remove it. Gurdit Singh sent messages to the king and the governor general and announced a hunger strike. On shore, Sikhs staged a large rally and were joined by the radical Socialist Party of Canada. An anti-Sikh rally quickly organized, addressed by MP Herbert Stevens: "The immigrant from northern Europe is highly desirable, the immigrant from southern Europe is much less so, and the Asiatic, and I wish to emphasize this, is entirely undesirable."

By June 20, the *Komagata Maru* had been sitting in Vancouver harbour for a month. Drinking water and food supplies were very low. Petitions came from the ship alleging starvation. Bagga Singh and the shore committee were furious at the deliberate starvation of passengers by the government. Members attempted to board the ship but were turned away.

The government played with the idea of kidnapping the *Komagata Maru* passengers and returning them to the Orient aboard a Canadian Pacific liner. Prime Minister Borden rejected the plan, afraid it might lead to bloodshed. Requests for fresh water were ignored by the immigration officials. Gurdit Singh sent another telegram to the governor general: "Many requests to the immigration department useless. Better to be shot than this miserable death."

Dissent put cracks in the common front of the *Komagata Maru*. Frightened, hungry Sikhs caved into the government's demand to select a single individual for a court test who would stand for all on board. Munshi Singh, a twenty-six-year-old married farmer, was chosen. Passengers gave up their single advantage: delay. The hundreds of cases would have taken many months to sort out and given defence lawyers a chance to pick apart the immigration regulations.

On June 28, the Board of Inquiry ruled Munshi Singh inadmissible. The case was appealed to five judges in Victoria and, on July 5, was lost. The legal battle was over. Gurdit Singh warned the governor general that the forcible return of the passengers would lead to agitation in India. He proposed that Sikhs be allowed to settle somewhere in the prairies. There was no reply.

A mutinous mood spread on board the *Komagata Maru*. The lack of water and food, the sickening stench of garbage, the cramped captivity gnawed at order. When the head of the immigration department went on board to inspect conditions, the Sikhs pounced and kept him hostage, only releasing him when Gurdit Singh intervened.

The immigration agent agreed the ship had to be cleaned up, mostly out of fear that an epidemic would start. The government also agreed to provide food and water for the return journey, but only after the ship had sailed to the three-mile limit. Suspecting a trick, the Sikhs declined. A week later the passengers were served with deportation orders and the captain was ordered out of the harbour. But the Sikhs had control of the ship.

The immigration officials hatched a plan: they would storm the *Komagata Maru,* subdue the passengers and sail the ship out to international waters. What followed became known as the Battle of Burrard Inlet.

Around one a.m. a force of 125 armed police officers and 35 special immigration agents, all armed with rifles, boarded the tug *Sea Lion,* accompanied by several newspapermen. When the Sea Lion arrived alongside the *Komagata Maru,* its deck was ten feet lower. The strike force was at a terrible disadvantage. Sikhs, four deep, manned the railing. Police flung grappling hooks on deck and used a high-pressure hose to scatter the opposition. The Punjabis hit back with lumps of coal, garbage, scrap metal and wood. Thirty people on the *Sea Lion* were injured, and the boat itself almost capsized. After ten minutes, the *Sea Lion* retreated. The *Sun* newspaper praised the police department's "admirable coolness and courage" and called the Punjabis "barbarians."

The Battle of Burrard Inlet was an embarrassing flop and the losers demanded retaliation. Prime Minister Borden played it both ways—sending his agricultural minister to negotiate while authorizing the use of the warship the HMCS *Rainbow* to intimidate the Sikhs. The next day the warship, half of Canada's navy, came alongside the *Komagata Maru*. Soldiers pointed their fixed bayonets at the unarmed passengers to frighten them into leaving. The Sikhs started reciting from the Guru Granth Sahib and fortified their courage with patriotic songs played on their sarangis—fiddles—and dhads, wooden drums. But the battle had been lost.

Food and medicine were brought on board, and on July 23, under the *Rainbow*'s escort, the *Komagata Maru* set sail out of Vancouver harbour. Not everyone noticed the irony that the Canadian navy was being used to stop British subjects from landing on British soil.

As the *Komagata Maru* steamed out of Burrard Inlet, hope left with it. Canada had not bowed to humanitarianism or to the plea of fellow subjects of the British Empire. Nor had it observed its own laws. Sovereignty had been enforced and perhaps even a notion of nationhood, independent of Britain. Indians were not welcome in Canada, and would not be for thirty-five more years. For Bagga Singh, it meant a long and painful wait to be reunited with his family.

The day of the *Komagata Maru*'s departure, the Governor of Hong Kong requested that the ship's passengers be refused landing for fear that they might incite Sikh regiments stationed in the British colony. They weren't allowed to land in Singapore, either. On September 29, the *Komagata Maru* docked at Budge Budge, near Calcutta, and the ship was surrounded by armed police. When the passengers disembarked, they were shoved toward the train station. The Sikhs resisted, sitting down at the rail crossing. They were immediately surrounded by police. As the police superintendent tried to arrest Gurdit Singh, the passengers moved in to protect him. In the massacre that followed, twenty Sikhs, two British officers, two Indian policemen and two local residents died. News of the event hardened anti-British sentiment in Punjab and in Canada. When war with Germany broke out later in the summer, militants urged Indians to come home and wage an armed uprising against the British. Hundreds of Sikhs left Canada, never to return.

Bagga Singh stayed, following the sawmill jobs in British Columbia. His community was dwindling without women or children, but by 1920 Sikhs had built temples in Vancouver, New Westminster, Victoria, Nanaimo, Golden, Abbotsford, Fraser Mills and Paldi, and owned six sawmills and two shingle mills. Still, the sting of exclusion followed Bagga for years. As he spit out sawdust from the mills, his wife raised their two children alone in Punjab. His daughters grew into young women and then married without ever knowing their father's love, unable to get into the country where he lived. After seventeen long years, Bagga Singh's wife, Harkaur, joined him in Canada; the government had loosened the regulations for children and spouses. Harkaur made the journey by boat through Hong Kong, following the path of the

Komagata Maru into Vancouver. Shortly after, they had another baby girl. Nsibe, their Canadian-born daughter.

Like so many Sikh workers, Bagga Singh hopscotched across the province for work, from the mainland to Paldi on Vancouver Island. Named after the mill owner's village in the Punjab, Paldi was the only town established by South Asians in Canada. Bagga finally settled down in New Westminster. The scent of lumber followed him and infused his daughter's life, the Canadian scent of cedar, Douglas fir, cypress, carried in her father's clothes. A smell his other children had never gotten to know.

For years Bagga Singh was paid less than white men for the same work, though it was still better than the wages in India. When the labour movement promised equality and better working conditions in the mills, South Asians joined up. The unions demanded justice not only in the workplace, but outside as well. At the same time, Bagga Singh's community quietly lobbied Ottawa. Fifty years after their arrival in Canada, they were finally given the right to vote, in April 1947.

Three generations of Sikhs have grown into citizenship since that first lonely generation of men made their lives here. Three generations of Canadians have prized their education and moved steadily into affluence. Bagga Singh's own granddaughter, Belle, studied journalism and became a local television reporter in a city that had once promised to keep its doors closed to Asians like her grandfather.

The *Komagata Maru* has long since faded into amnesia and Dominion Hall is now an art studio. But within those walls is the ghost of a dark-skinned man, bearded and turbaned, who made a plea for social conscience and justice. While he worked and lived invisibly, forever "other" and apart, Bagga Singh, the sawmill worker, challenged the very foundations of Canadian law, and worked for its equal application for all. It is an idea now enshrined in the Canadian constitution, an idea that Bagga brought to Canada before its time.

Bagga Singh died in 1954, at the age of sixty-three. But his searing sense of inclusion, hard won by a faith that had itself risen from the wounds of injustice half a world away, helped make a new nation more just.

South Asian Immigration History in Canada

The first Sikh in Canada was probably Prince Victor Duleep Singh, grandson of Maharja Ranjit Singh, "the Lion of the Punjab." In 1889 he joined Sir John Ross, commander of the Imperial Forces in Canada, as aide de camp at his headquarters in Halifax. He was a second lieutenant in the first Royal Dragoons. Eight years later, a group of Sikh troops came through Canada on their way to Queen Victoria's Diamond Jubilee celebrations in London.

But the Canadian public's first real glimpse of Sikhs was in 1902. Sikhs with the Hong Kong military contingent travelled to the coronation of Edward VII. Crossing Canada to and from England, they astonished Canadians with their exotic appearance and military professionalism. These soldiers returned to India with stories of a land waiting to be settled by British subjects like themselves.

More than 5,000 South Asians, over ninety percent of them Sikhs, came to British Columbia before their immigration was banned in 1908. From then on, the population gradually dwindled to about 2,000 through out-migration. Almost all of those remaining were Sikhs.

Despite profound discrimination, Sikhs quickly established a strong community in British Columbia, the centre of which was their religious institutions. The Vancouver Khalsa Diwan Society was created in 1907. Through its leadership Sikhs built their first permanent *gurdwara,* or temple, the following year. By 1920, *gurdwaras* had been established in New Westminster, Victoria, Nanaimo, Golden, Abbotsford, Fraser Mills and Paldi.

The Canadian Sikh community developed around the *gurdwaras*. It was through the *gurdwaras* that Sikhs provided support and aid to community members in need. These temples organized the Sikh communities in their dramatic fight to have the immigration ban rescinded. By 1920 Sikhs in Vancouver alone had contributed $300,000 to charitable causes in India and to the defence of Sikhs in Canada.

Canadian Sikh religious institutions grew considerably when wives and children of legal Sikh residents were allowed into Canada in the 1920s. Entire families—men, women and children—all participated fully in both temple and home observances.

Sikh religion also provided the foundation for a strong collective community identity between World War I and World War II. Very few Sikhs renounced their faith in favour of assimilating into the Canadian society, and very few married outside the Sikh community. The main religious change during the period from 1920 to 1960, however, was a trend among second generation Sikh men to become *sahajdharis*, which involved cutting their hair and beards that had traditionally been left to grow long, and conforming to Canadian dress.

The Sikh community and Sikhism in Canada was revitalized when immigration resumed in the 1950s. Many postwar immigrants were more urbane, educated, westernized and religiously untraditional than those who had come before. In the 1960s and 1970s tens of thousands of skilled Sikhs settled across Canada, especially in southern Ontario from Toronto to Windsor. As the size of the

Canadian Sikh community grew, *gurdwaras* were established in every major city east of Montreal.

In 1991, census figures estimated that there were 145,000 Sikhs in Canada, but this is considered to be somewhat low. Population estimates at the end of 1993 put the size of the Sikh population in Canada closer to 180,000.

Overcoming Obstacles

Like many Indian immigrants who arrived in Canada at the turn of the century, Bagga Singh came across the United States border, forced to manoeuvre around the immigration laws that were designed to keep people like him out. Admission of South Asians to Canada had gone unrestricted until 1908, when a ban was imposed on all Asian immigration.

Mackenzie King, then labour minister, claimed, "The Hindu is not suited to the climate of this country." In 1909 the government of British Columbia took away the rights of Indians to vote—a right that should have been guaranteed by the fact that they were British subjects, like all other Canadians.

In 1914, the Indian community faced an insurmountable challenge with the arrival of a shipload of Sikh immigrants. As the *Komagata Maru* lingered for two months off Vancouver, waiting for permission to land its passengers, the Indian Canadian community was galvanized into action. The *Komagata Maru* was eventually forced back into international waters, but Canadian Sikhs continued their efforts to negotiate an end to the immigration ban and better social conditions in their new country.

South Asian Canadians faced pervasive discrimination in Canadian society. Without the right to vote they could no longer enter professions or secure government contracts or good jobs. For decades, Indians like Bagga Singh were paid less than white men for the same work. Despite the hardships, Canada still offered better opportunities than India, and hard work did pay off. When the labour movement promised equality and better working conditions in the sawmills, Indians joined up.

The unions demanded equality not only in the workplace but outside as well—where Indians encountered "Whites Only" signs at theatres and restaurants, and resistance to their purchasing homes in certain areas.

Even if they'd been allowed to buy homes, they would have been empty most of the time. Indian families were rarely allowed to join their men in Canada. The Indian community, 6,000 strong, was primarily a bachelor society. It wasn't until the 1920s that wives and children of legal Sikh residents were finally allowed to enter the country.

In 1947, fifty years after their arrival in Canada, Indians were finally given the right to vote, along with Chinese-Canadians. Shortly after, in the 1950s, the immigration ban was lifted and immigration resumed.

The Indian-Canadian Legacy

After seventeen long years, Bagga Singh's wife, Harkaur, joined him in Canada. Soon after they had a third daughter, Nsibe. For Bagga Singh, as with Indian-Canadians in general, family ties and a sense of community were important parts of a full and prosperous life. They provided safe harbour against stinging racism and supplied the foundations for economic prosperity.

Over the decades, many Indian families grew and prospered. A century after their arrival, some Indians continue to work in the lumber mills, many of them now owning the mills where their fathers and grandfathers toiled. Bagga Singh moved across the province in search of work, from the mainland to Paldi on Vancouver Island. Paldi is named after mill owner Mal Singh's village in the Punjab and is the one town established by Indians in Canada.

In 1947, four months after Indians received the right to vote in Canada, the British left India and gave the colony its independence. Celebrations went on around the world. In Canada, Bagga Singh, now a proud full-fledged citizen, must have rejoiced at India getting its freedom.

The Canadian Sikh community is still strongly affected by events concerning Sikhs and Sikhism in India. One central issue since the 1970s has been the rise of a nationalist movement in the Punjab for greater Sikh rights and for an independent Sikh state. Continued attention and involvement with Indian issues has affected Sikh religious practice in Canada. Heightened Sikh consciousness has led to a remarkable increase in Amritdharis and Keshdharis, even among second- and third-generation Canadians.

With its strong community institutions and group consciousness, Sikhism has found fertile ground in Canada and the community has resisted pressures to assimilate. With continued immigration and the rise of a large second generation, it is estimated that Canadian Sikhs will number 200,000 by the year 2000.

Sources

Canadian Sikhs, Narindar Singh. Canadian Sikhs' Studies Institute, Ottawa.

The East Indians in Canada, Hugh Johnston. Canadian Historical Association, 1984.

The Fitzhenry & Whiteside Book of Canadian Facts & Dates, Jay Myers. Fitzhenry & Whiteside, Richmond Hill, 1991.

Passage from India, directed by Ali Kazimi. Produced by White Pine Pictures, Toronto, 1998.

Sikhism: A Resource Book for Teachers, Dr. Mohinder Singh. Sikh Education.

The Voyage of the Komagata Maru: The Sikh Challenge to Canada's Colour Bar, Hugh Johnston. Oxford University Press, Toronto, 1979.

Bob and Jane Aberson

Chapter Ten
The Magnificent Abersons

Canada and the World in 1924

The Royal Canadian Air Force is established.

The B.C. legislature adopts a resolution opposing the continued immigration of Oriental people to Canada.

Parliament passes the United Church of Canada Act, joining Methodists, Presbyterians and Congregationalists together to form the largest Protestant church in Canada.

Albania and Greece are proclaimed republics.

Adolf Hitler, who would later lead Germany as leader of the Nazi Party, is sentenced to five years' imprisonment for trying to overthrow the government.

Calvin Coolidge wins the U.S. election for president.

E.M. Forester writes *A Passage to India.*

George Bernard Shaw writes *St. Joan.*

Vladimir Lenin, one of the founders of communism, who was instrumental in the Russian Revolution of 1917, dies.

Aspirin tablets, enclosed cars, Band-Aids, clip-on bowties, elastic brassieres, sliced bread, bubble gum, cellophane-wrapped packages, cigarette lighters, packaged detergents, electric hair dryers, Kleenex, Kotex, electric ovens, phonographs and radios, liquid shampoo, tea bags, one-piece telephones, canned tomato juice and Yo-Yos become widely available in the 1920s.

Jane Aberson grew up in the low-clouded lowlands of Holland, craving a big sky and the searing definiteness of other geographies. She wanted adventure in an untamed place. Jane had never peeled a carrot, let alone cooked one—there were servants for that. But she was determined to escape the dull dampness of home and privilege, and to feel the world on her skin. Then she got engaged to the boy next door.

Bob Aberson had the same adventurous itch as Jane, and the same urge to get out of Holland. The Great War had just ended and Europe was bloodied and weary. It was time to grab hold of a dream. Bob hurtled to a bank job in Jakarta, on the island of Java, and Jane went racing after him. They hurried through a marriage without any of their relatives, and aimed themselves at their exotic fantasy. It was the wrong part of the world.

The Dutch East Indies was one of the last remnants of Holland's colonial power and old glories hung over the tropics like a dank shadow. Servants scurried for drinks and the Dutch remembered their victories over the Asiatic, their colonies in South Africa, Ceylon and New York. They'd even claimed Acadia once. The Abersons choked on the tedium and Bob detested office work. He developed an interest in agriculture and a Dutch colony was no place to get his hands dirty.

Back in Holland, the Abersons laid startled eyes on a billboard advertising Canada. "Welcome to Winnipeg and Manitoba's boundless wheatfields." It was a beautiful picture of a clean, new place that looked like a modern Eden: a field of wheat, a happy farmer and a wife with a baby in her arms. A welcoming wave from the New World, made by some of the best propaganda artists in Canada. It was the century that belonged to Canada and Bob and Jane were smitten.

For twenty years the Dominion, desperate for settlers, had dangled its picture-perfect self like bait into the world, luring immigrants: free land, good land, homeland, your land. The advertising plan started with Manitoba politician and former interior minister Clifford Sifton. He'd ordered full-page promotions in foreign newspapers, along with billboards and millions of multi-language pamphlets. It worked. Immigrants started jumping into boats like cod off the Grand Banks. In the first decade of the new century, the Canadian population increased from 5,000,000 to 7,000,000, most of the newcomers heading to the prairies as farmers.

But Bob was trained in trade and commerce, his family argued, not farming, for goodness sake. He'd never had a shovel in his hands. "You are a bank man. You must be very strong to be a farmer." "Well, I am strong," he told them. "I play tennis," and showed them his arm.

Canada was exactly what the Abersons wanted—a place to roll up their sleeves and live by their muscle and wit, something to be earned, not inherited. They made inquiries at the Department of Emigration in The Hague. "We do not see anything feasible in your plans to start farming," an official wrote back. "You do not have the background, the know-how and, most likely, not the stamina to become farmers. We advise you strongly to forget these plans and go back to the work for which you were trained."

It was a stinging rebuke that hardened their resolve. The Abersons organized their lives around leaving. Bob's passport was still good, so he could go alone and get a head start on their new life. Jane would stay home with their toddler. Bob booked a passage to Canada and headed for Manitoba.

Bob Aberson worked for $1 a day as a hired man and studied at the agricultural college in Winnipeg. He soaked up everything he could about wheat—King Wheat they called it, prairie gold, fifty million bushels of the stuff produced a year. It shaped the whole economy, Bob discovered. Insurance companies scheduled their premium payments for the first day of November, when farmers were flush with their cashed-in crops; children were named Garnet and Marquis after the kinds of grain that had helped pay down their family's homestead mortgage.

When winter set in, Bob was still wearing his tropical gear from Java. Out on Portage Avenue in Winnipeg the cold was so painful, he scurried into a public washroom and wrapped toilet paper around his legs for insulation. He wrote letters to Jane warning her about the raw conditions. She'd better prepare herself to go back in history about 100 years, he told her; there was little electricity and running water on Canadian farms. Jane's mind swelled with excited imaginings. When Bob finally wrote that he'd found them a little place in the bush near Dauphin, his wife was eager to join him.

A year after Bob's departure, Jane and little Bob Jr. lugged their steamer trunks across the Atlantic and then on to a train to Dauphin. Their mouths fell open at the huge land around them. Here was the big adventure Jane Aberson had hankered for: mile after mile of land, trees and wheat, and a stretched-out sky. It made her blink. The bareness of the land was eerie—only a house or two clustered along the track. They looked so run down, not like the pictures in the immigration posters. Jane thought they'd been abandoned. But the homes weren't old. They'd been built by people dropped off the very same train Jane was travelling on. They too had been left gaping on the bald prairie, clutching little more than tools and grain seed. Some had stacked together sod houses, others had made log homes or tar-paper shacks.

For a year Jane had prepared little Bobby Jr. for going to Canada and seeing his father, trying hard to keep her husband's memory alive. When they arrived in Dauphin, the stranger on the platform moved toward them. "Do you know who this is?" Jane asked the boy. Bobby stared up, squinting at the man. "That's Canada." The family laughed and held on to each other. Then Bob took his wife and boy to their own little home.

Jane had never seen a more desolate place. The weeds grew wild around the log cabin, tall as a man. The house itself was leaning in the wind. The chinking between the logs had fallen out in places. With Jane standing inside and Bob outside, the couple shook hands through the walls, laughing uproariously about the "airiness" of the place.

Jane was flushed with optimism. The primitive and isolated cabin suited her sense of adventure. So did the deer and elk watching from the bush. She and Bob pranced around like Adam and Eve, running to the river for their baths, while baby Bobby shrieked in the commotion.

It took a few weeks to claim the cabin and make it home. Jane laid out her small assortment of rugs and keepsakes from Holland while Bob dragged in second-hand furniture. They were probably the only people on the prairies to hang batik sarongs from the Dutch East Indies over their rough log walls. Jane sniped a little about the outhouse and having to pump every drop of hard water, but river water was just a few hundred yards from the house. Home was now a clearing of about thirty acres where Bob farmed. In the log cabin, Jane looked sourly at the sloping add-on called a kitchen, and at the old stove and washtub.

Summer scorched the prairies and demanded a furious physical effort. Jane could feel the country bulging with anticipation as grain crops grew. A good yield, a good grade, were the longed-for words hiding in conversations. Bob put his back into the land alongside the homesteaders, and the farmers' wives showed Jane how to make preserves and pickles. Canadians, she discovered, loved their pickles. Everywhere, the kindness of hands were offered up. Men and women counted on their neighbours here, and neighbours rarely counted the favours. Bob and Jane heard their low grumblings, too, and their contempt for bigwigs. Farmers hated the central Canadians who controlled the high freight rates of the CPR, and the Winnipeg grain barons who lived in mansions on Wellington Crescent and siphoned off too much profit. Farmers had retaliated by pooling their own wheat. Just that year, the three prairie provinces combined their pools to create the Central Selling Agency with offices overseas. They'd soon be handling half the prairie wheat crop—forty percent of the world's total export.

Jane loved the place, and the fierceness and fairness of farmers. They weren't a single people like in Holland, but strangers from all over the world, negotiating the land and each other. Thousands were still arriving, crowding out the French and Métis. By the turn of the century, mostly English-speaking transplants from Ontario had already moved in, settling lands south of the CPR's main line. Smaller groups of French, Icelander and Mennonites had coalesced around them, then Eastern Europeans from the Ukraine and Poland. Other nation's names were written on prairie towns—the French Beausejour and Dauphin; the Icelandic Arbakka and Gimli; the Scottish Argyle; Ukraina from the Ukraine; and Clandeboye from Ireland. It was a remarkable human layering that worked because the exigencies of the land forced it to. And because a second chance reaffirmed faith in goodness. Hope is a social adhesive.

Winter arrived with a sudden stillness—a slow, crawling time that lasted six months in Canada, Jane discovered. After a summer of work and the harvest rush, farmers put their feet up the first weeks of freeze-up. Jane struggled with winter laundry, learning to melt snow for wash water and to get the clothes dry. If she hung them outside, they hardened like icicles. Another time, a strong wind blew them to bits. Finally, she put a line up in a washshed. She also learned to avoid frozen doorknobs. Time after time she reached for the metal with a damp hand and got stuck to it. Many layers of skin were torn off in the process of remembering.

From her first week, Jane faithfully described her daily life in letters home. Family and friends were astounded at the details they'd never heard about in the immigration literature: "The fences and the shrubs, like the lilacs and raspberries, have all disappeared under the snow. Our mailbox, which reaches to our shoulders, is now level with the ground. The mailman needs to get out of his sleigh and get down on his hands and knees for our mail. He says we will need to dig the snow away from the mailbox or he won't deliver our mail anymore."

For her family back in Holland, it would always be a source of wonder that Jane, the girl who'd never learned to cook or use a vacuum cleaner, who'd been waited on by servants, was surviving a pioneer life in the Canadian west. And loving it.

Only Christmas turned her heart homeward. Christmas *was* Holland. The yearly arrival of Saint Nicholas, the patron saint of children and of gift giving, the original Santa Claus, was a Dutch tradition. As a girl, Jane used to imagine the good saint riding on his white horse over the roofs, followed by his faithful black helper, Zwarte Piet, stuffing the wooden shoes of good children with treats. But this jolly old Canadian man in the red suit called Santa Claus seemed too clownish to Jane, and one-dimensional. As the Aberson family grew and two more sons, Wim and Dirk, arrived, Jane made sure they celebrated both

Christmases. The children, with typical boyish mischief, filled each other's shoes with presents from the horse barn. Jane reported home: "Our boys are no longer Dutch children. They are young Canadians who generally need to be reminded to answer back in the Dutch language once in a while. So they don't forget Dutch altogether. To them the jolly Santa Claus is the height of ecstasy!"

For Jane, the big treat was a trip to Winnipeg, where she visited the holy shrines of department stores, the Hudson's Bay and T. Eaton companies. It was far more delectable than buying from the "Farmer's Bible"—the catalogue. Jane would get a quick snack in the cafeteria or, if she was really feeling flush, splurge on a fine meal on the top floor where she could see the whole city.

Sometimes she and Bob would tour the town and Jane gaped at the fancy houses with the thrill of a child looking through a candy-shop window. These were the homes of the grain barons, Bob reminded her, who'd gambled on the grain exchange with *their* crops and made a fortune. Jane could see the contrast between their grand houses and the homes of people like her who actually grew the grain. She felt a twinge of spite. She wasn't alone—resentment was spreading across the west.

The crash of 1929 was blistering. The farmers' own wheat pools, which had steered clear of the futures markets, collapsed as the price of grain plummeted, and banks foreclosed on mortgages. In the first years of the Dirty Thirties, grade-one wheat went down to forty then thirty-five cents a bushel. In Dauphin, the Abersons were paying seventeen cents a bushel in freight charges. When rain lowered wheat quality by one grade, the difference was four cents a bushel. Subtracting the cost of threshing, labour and binder-twine, the farmers had nothing left but debt.

Jane wrote it all down in her letters home. They were read voraciously and circulated among her family. One of her uncles, a language teacher in Groningen, told her that she should publish them in the newspaper. "No, I'm just a housewife," she wrote back. The uncle went to the management of the *Nieuwsblad van het Noorden* (The Northern Daily) in Holland, which immediately wanted to print them. Later Jane would recall how she made her decision:

> We soon began to realize that making a living in Canada on a small farm was far from easy. Prices were low, crops did not always come up to expectations, and many of the ventures we embarked on with livestock often proved disappointing. Suddenly the thought of making a few extra dollars writing about life in Canada looked very appealing. By this time I had really started to love the country, but I wanted to get even with that misleading picture we had seen on the poster in The Hague. Canada was a wonderful country and needed no extra embellishments. So I made up my mind to describe things in the way we saw them ourselves.

Jane's letters began appearing in the Dutch paper every Saturday, selling a few thousand, and even five and six thousand more copies. On special occasions, like

Christmas, when she wrote heartwarming pieces, the newspaper sold 50,000 copies more. In a matter of months, Jane had become a minor celebrity in Holland. In Canada, she was still a farmer's wife and a mother, an identity that infused her columns for the Dutch newspaper.

> In the pasture, against the sunny river bank, the sheep nurse their new lambs which arrive every day. A few clucking hens, followed by a flock of baby chicks scuttle over the yard...
>
> In between the lambs and the chickens our three sons roll in the grass, not knowing which prank to pull next out of sheer exuberance. Bobby, who celebrated his tenth birthday a few days ago, received a box of firecrackers from a school pal and scared the wits out of us only ten minutes ago, by sneaking some under our chairs and awaiting the results from a safe distance. Who would not be tempted to pull pranks on a lovely day like this?

The Abersons were hard-working farmers, and their enthusiasm was irrepressible. They were also the brunt of good-natured jokes. Neighbours thought they were green and impractical, especially when Bob dried his wheat stooks upside down. Then one summer's evening, sitting on their front lawn with friends, Bob reminisced about the tennis he used to play in Holland. Maybe they should build a tennis court. They thought of the cost and the idea withered from the conversation. But Jane couldn't get it out of her head. "Are you crazy? A tennis court on the farm?" Bob objected. Local opinion was behind him. "We must use every inch of this country for wheat and potatoes and what else you grow as a farmer. Tennis, that's a luxury!" Jane thought it would be great for the community. So up the court went, despite the nudges, winks and whispers of neighbours.

The three Aberson boys saw the potential right away. Bobby, Wim and Dirk thought it would make a great skating rink. It wasn't long before tennis season was over and they were hauling water from the river and flooding the court. The only things missing were hockey sticks and pucks. But they were make-do, can-do Canadian farm boys—they used horse buns and willow sticks. The tennis court endeared Jane to the locals. In the pared-down, pragmatic ways of the prairies, in the dirt poor, dust days of the Depression, there was something magnificent, if not a little strange, about indulging in the luxury of a dream.

Over the years Jane mastered the art of farm survival, tending her garden and raising as many as 200 chickens, 70 turkeys and 17 geese. She transfixed her Dutch readers with her daily ordeals, describing how the chamber pots were frozen over on winter mornings, the hallway full of snow that had to be swept out. Jane wrote about warming up the house with two roaring stoves and making breakfast with frozen butter and meat while Bob did the milking.

Now the boys come downstairs, each with a bundle of clothes under his arm. Shivering, they crowd around the stove. "Hurry up!" I shout. "Out of your pajamas.

> You only have half an hour left." They start to dawdle. "My hands are so cold I can't manage these buttons." "My moccasins are hard as a board."
>
> Bob comes into the house with full milk pails. Big chunks of snow, mixed with manure, stick to his rubber boots and start to melt over the floor. I look at it with venom. All the same I know that it is practically impossible to scrape off all that frozen stuff outside. However it does not improve my temper. What's the use trying to keep the floor decently clean?

Her Dutch readers were enthralled. Children would lie in their homes on Saturdays, reading her "Van de Canadeesche Velden"—"From the Canadian Fields"—wanting to grow up to be like Jane, to do what she did.

Strangers started arriving at the Aberson homestead, a continuous stream of Dutch immigrants who knew Jane, or thought they did, through her articles. They'd been inspired by her to come to Canada, and had promised themselves to make the effort to get to Manitoba and meet her. Jane entertained the wanderers, while writing her columns and doing the chores. But everything and everyone was cast aside for harvesting. The hardest days of the year, and the most dreaded, were threshing days.

Threshing gangs roamed from farm to farm. They always arrived the night before, rattling in with their caboose—the trailer the men slept in. Wagons, tractors and the threshing machine rumbled along behind. At least twenty extra men expected to be fed the whole hard days ahead. They were farmers' sons, Hungarians, Ukrainians, natives, big men with big stomachs. Food was the high point of their day and nothing spooked farm women more than the stories about gangs threatening to strike because they didn't like what was served.

The Abersons always cleared out their house the night before, leaving only the tables and chairs. Then they both got up at half past three. While Bob sweated with the threshing gang under the scorching sun, Jane worked alone in the kitchen. Breakfast was served at five a.m. sharp: potatoes, rolled oats, bacon and eggs, four loaves of bread, canned fruit, and two platters of cakes. Jane recorded her thoughts for her readers in Holland: "Whoever heard of cake for breakfast? Did I forget anything now? Oh, sure enough! They have to have pickles. Without pickles it would not be a Canadian meal. Canadians serve pickles even with tea."

The dishes were washed, more food prepared, pies baked, children fed and sent to school, then dinner at eleven o'clock. After that, another dirty heap of dishes to wash. Jane would lift her head briefly, squinting into the sun where the dust billowed up from the threshing machine: "I look out over the field again and see it bathed in brilliant sunshine. What a privileged country with so much sunshine! The men are making good headway in the field. Most of the wheat stooks have already disappeared."

Then she bent back into her work—boxing lunches to be served from the running board of the car at four p.m. and rumbling across the stubbled fields with a kettle of scalding hot tea at her feet. Jane served the last meal at eight, the weary crowd lingering while she breathed down their necks. "Hurry up, please hurry up," she'd plead silently, her body more machine than flesh, her mind numb. She had to get to bed so she could get up early the next day to do it all over again. And then finally the work would be over:

> These exhilarating days are the crown of a whole year's work. The black spook of very low prices is pushed aside for the moment. That disenchantment will come later....When tranquillity has returned we estimate our profit and loss for the year. "If only we could get a decent price," sighed Bob...
>
> We finished by taking a stroll in the garden. The tomatoes were hanging in heavy clusters on the vines and quite a few have started to colour. The corn was also ripening, as the tassels were getting dark. Corn is a vegetable that we did not know about in Holland, but here it is very popular.
>
> "Well," we said to each other, "we will not starve this winter, whatever the prices may be." A cellar full of our own produce, vegetables as well as poultry and other meat, is at least something to show for a busy summer!

In early 1936, Jane and Bob sat at the dining-room table of their newly built home, marvelling at the wonders of modern technology. They were listening to the funeral of King George V, broadcast live around the world on radio. Voices crackled through the speaker. "By the grace of God, King of Great Britain, Ireland and the British dominions across the sea..." The King of England was being carried to his grave and a faraway death was brought close. It was only a few months later that Jane was diagnosed with cancer.

The doctors told Bob there wasn't much more they could do to help her. The prognosis was grim. But there was a specialist in Holland and Jane hurried across the sea. It was the first time she'd been home in twelve years, the first time she'd been that long away from her boys. Jane underwent a series of operations over the winter that shrank the cancer. It never reappeared. While she was recuperating, she was coaxed into a lecture tour. The newspaper did the advertising and publicity for her, and to her amazement, every time she went to speak, she was greeted by a full hall of people, standing room only, eager to hear about Canada.

She was never paid much, ten Dutch cents per word she wrote, and not much more for the lectures. When she got home she bought two bicycles for her sons with her small earnings, second-hand ones because there wasn't enough money for new ones.

The neighbours were quietly impressed that someone from Dauphin had gone overseas to speak. But Jane avoided the fanfare. She got on with her chores and her garden, and sometimes, a drive in the car and a Saturday night out.

> Farmers do not have very fancy cars. They are old boxes on wheels, with flapping and often torn tops.

They shake and rattle but get you where you want to go, and that's the main thing. If we can find somebody to look after the children we leave them at home when we go to town, but mostly, to their great delight, of course, we have to take them to town with us. When the children, fresh from their baths, have been put into clean clothes, when the cattle have been looked after, the house has been tidied and we ourselves are dressed, our little old Ford drives out of the gate to take us to town.

Dauphin was a snoozy place, blinking awake every weekend. Strings of coloured lights hung across Main Street, and the shops were lit up until eleven. Farmers started arriving after their chores, promenading along the street or clustering in bunches against the buildings. Jane and Bob always tried to park on Main Street, preferably in front of the drug store, where a radio or gramophone pumped out music every Saturday night. Then they'd sit back in the Ford and guess the nationalities of the passersby.

If you have your ears open you realize how many nationalities populate Canada. In front of the big grocery store a group of women with dark or coloured head shawls talk as much with their hands as with their lips. I can't make out a word because it is likely Ukrainian, or perhaps Russian or Polish. Among this group you'll also find young girls with hats fashionably worn at an angle, makeup on their faces, and

> smart Eaton's catalogue dresses. The young East European generation does not want to wear the head shawls of their elders.

Over by the post office another knot of men was huddled in furious conversation, hands darting out in exclamation. These were the French, only they spoke too fast for Jane to understand: "Of course, you can hear English in different dialects, from the unmusical 'knauw knauw' of the Americans to the unadulterated English of a Cockney, the distinctive brogue of the Scots and the musical whimsy of the Irish."

Invariably, their own language wafted toward them, and a few suited Dutch men would tug at Bob to go for a drink. Women and children weren't allowed in beer parlours, nor could they even glimpse their men through the windows. Manitoba law had drawn a curtain across the public consumption of alcohol and entertainment. Beer parlours and dance halls were shuttered from the public, windows draped or frosted, shrouding the goings-on in naughty secrecy. It wasn't at all like the sidewalk cafes of Jane's girlhood.

Farm women had their own "Ladies' Rest Room" to retire to, a sad little place in a basement without a view, run by the United Farm Women of Manitoba. A supervisor watched over their parcels and children's dirty hands could be washed there. But women preferred the grocery stores and Eaton's, or the thirty-five-cent picture show where talkies were now the rage: "A few years ago we could only see silent films, during which a woman played an organ. She imitated galloping horses and murmuring brooks to perfection, and Bob always liked the music better than the show."

Jane enjoyed the Chinese cafe, a clean, cheap place where she sat in a boxed stall and ordered a full meal with soup and dessert for thirty-five cents.

At 10:45 last call sent a tremor through the men at the beer parlour, and they hurried to order as many glasses as their tables could bear. By eleven, the town lights flickered out and women eyed the crowds sourly for their husbands. Bags of provisions were dragged into cars and put on the backseat where children were sleeping. As Dauphin leaned back into its own dreams, carts, buggies and cars sped out of town into the dark and dust of country roads.

But across the sea, the old country was beginning to hemorrhage.

In May 1940, German troops crossed the Dutch frontier and paratroopers fell into the west. Holland was occupied by the Nazis. Here, in the land of Anne Frank, the roundup of Jews began. The Germans grew increasingly ruthless, and in the last hard winter, cornered by the Allies, they brutalized the Dutch. It was called the Hunger Winter; the Dutch were starving, eating tulip bulbs and breaking buildings to burn the wood. Families roamed the countryside scavenging for food. Queen Wilhelmina's daughter Juliana sought refuge in Ottawa, and gave birth to a daughter there. The Dutch Diaspora agonized, listening to their radios for news of home.

When Jane heard of the deprivation of her countrymen, she started a fundraising campaign by holding garden parties. Ladies from Dauphin and the surrounding area attended. It was considered a very prestigious social event to go to Mrs. Aberson's tea parties. The women talked mostly about the war; a lot of them had brothers and sons overseas. Some of their men would end up marching into Holland and pushing the Germans out. The Dutch fought mightily against the enemy. So did Canadians.

On May 25, 1945, the German troops finally surrendered to Canadian Commander General Charles Foulkes. Canada had liberated Holland. The Dutch scrambled onto their tanks, laughing for the first time in five years. Canadian soldiers handed out chocolate bars and soap to a tired, hungry people. In gratitude, the Dutch sent tulip bulbs every year after, to be planted in Ottawa at the annual Tulip Festival.

Jane went back to Holland after the war—her articles had been published in a book, which was selling out. The newspaper organized 120 lectures and Jane spoke five nights a week to standing-room crowds. Bob joined her, manning the projector. The war-weary Dutch weighed her every word, trying to imagine themselves on the prairies, working up the courage. Jane must have seen her own face staring back at her, the same earnest dream to begin again after an awful war. She gave them hope, not the poetic kind, but the pragmatic, explaining the other landscapes of Canada. She told them about bank policies and schools, about doctors and droughts, department stores and Chinese cafes. She wrote lovingly about the other dreamers who had settled the country alongside her, explaining the hard-knuckled ways of farm life and the epiphanies of motherhood and good neighbourliness. She was Canada's best ambassador.

> We were brought up in a carefree financial circumstances, which greatly influenced our outlook on life on this side of the ocean. What others might consider as a hardship we often saw as a big adventure, some tall tale to write home about. I will not say that we did not have difficult times, but the contrast and the adventure of life on the prairies made it an experience we would not like to have missed. We learned to love Canada and its people and have never been sorry we made the move.

For many of the invisible Dutch who blended so inconspicuously into Canada, Jane Aberson was their own voice, in their own language, speaking about the real Canada. Refusing the sugar coating of propaganda because the country didn't need it, Jane was the chronicler of a new nation, and its interpreter. It would take English-speaking Canadians many more decades to discover her and to celebrate her love for a country that belonged to them all. In 1979 she translated her letters and stories into English with Bob. She published her book *From the Prairies with Hope* mostly for her three boys, so that they could read it in a language they understood.

Jane Aberson died in 1998, leaving a permanent legacy of wit and wonder for generations of Canadians. Despite her naive expectations of a country she knew so little about, she delighted in its mysteries and pioneered a life that was remarkable for its unpretentiousness and common sense. It is the hallmark of what we now recognize as the prairie character. Jane Aberson discovered the extraordinary in ordinary Canadian farm life, and shared the rarest of human blessings: contentment. She had known, as far back as 1933, that she was living out her dream.

> I found a picture the other day in a magazine. There was a big field of heather, all purple with the purple sky stretching over it. And in the distance was the figure of a young girl in a red skirt and white blouse sitting in the midst of all those colourful blossoms. That picture put me right back into the past to when I was a high school girl bicycling over the heather trails with my school friends in the Netherlands. We would lie on our backs stretched out on the spongy moss underneath, soaking in all the beauty around us and dream our lovely dreams. Standing in the kitchen, staring at the picture and thinking about all those wonderful dreams, I realized I was now standing in the very room I was once dreaming about. It was not the kind of home I'd visualized then, but the afternoon sun was now hitting the frozen window pane and the room was becoming nice and cosy again....I am so glad Bob and I wound up in Canada after all.

Dutch Immigration History in Canada

The Dutch arrived in North America in the seventeenth century and by 1626 had established a colony on Manhattan Island they called New Amsterdam. Then they began making raids and claims on Acadia. In 1674 the Dutch privateer, Jurriaen Aernoutsz, captured Pentagouet, and took Governor Jacques de Chambly prisoner. After plundering the French posts along the Bay of Fundy, he claimed Acadia for Holland. But it wasn't until the American Revolution that Dutch American Loyalists settled in the British North American colonies. Already considerably anglicized, this group was quickly assimilated into the existing society and masses of immigrants who flooded into the colonies after 1815.

The Dutch came to Canada in three main waves. The first settlers arrived in Canada between 1890 and 1914, dreaming of prosperity and peace. The Netherlands was in the middle of a revolution in the last decade of the nineteenth century, as a predominantly rural and agricultural society transformed into an urban, industrial one. Social changes were immense and economic disparities rose up between people; poverty, crime, industrial pollution and exploitation were rampant. The North American frontier offered a fresh start, but cheap land had become scarce in the United States. The Dutch and Dutch-Americans turned to Canada as the "last best West." Since then, about 200,000 Dutch immigrants have settled in Canada. The Dutch quickly adopted Canadian culture and traditions, and have been integrated almost to the point of invisibility.

The first Dutch immigrants were encouraged to homesteads and railway lands in the Canadian west, to help cultivate and open up the prairies. They scattered across the plains as farmhands, farmers or ranch owners. The Dutch established ethnic settlements in New Nijverdal, now Monarch, Neerlandia in Alberta, and Edam in Saskatchewan. They also settled around Calgary, Edmonton and Winnipeg, which had the largest Dutch community in Canada prior to WW I.

In 1917 the Department of Immigration and Colonization was created, expecting that immigrants would come flooding into Canada during the postwar years. The country needed suitable immigrants and sent its immigration agents into Europe with glowing descriptions of free or cheap land, jobs and success guaranteed for the hardworking. Bob and Jane Aberson saw a large billboard with a picture of a farm in Canada. As Jane remembered in her book, "It was extremely tempting." The Abersons arrived during the second wave of Dutch immigration, between 1920 and 1930.

Cheap land was less available for this group of immigrants, but there was a big demand for farm, construction and industrial or domestic labour, particularly as the postwar recession came to an end. Dutch immigrants eagerly took up opportunities, particularly in central and western Canada. Large numbers concentrated in southern and southwestern Ontario, and in Toronto. Between 1890 and 1930, an estimated 25,000 Dutch or Dutch-Americans entered Canada.

The Depression and WW II slowed Dutch immigration to Canada, but by 1947 a kind of emigration fever grabbed hold of the Netherlands. It had a lot to do with Canada's role there during the war. Of all the fronts Canada operated in, the liberation of Holland stands as one of this nation's finest hours. While the Americans moved into the Netherlands in 1944, and British troops liberated the southern part, it was the Canadians who made the final push to clear the region between the Maas and Rhine rivers and to shove the Nazis out. Canadians freed western Holland, including the major cities of Amsterdam, Rotterdam and the Dutch capital, The Hague. What they found were Dutch starving from the worst winter of the war. The people of Holland cheered their liberators, and the "Canadian summer" that followed carved a deep bond between the two nations. Of the 42,000 Canadians who died during WW II, more than a quarter of them fell during that final Battle of the Rhine. Holland never forgot our courage, nor the fact that we had protected their future Queen Juliana in exile in Ottawa during the war years. They tend the graves of our dead with care and thoughtfulness, and every year the royal family of Holland and its tulip producers send 25,000 tulip bulbs to Ottawa. They bloom yearly for the Tulip Festival, a reminder of friendship. And of hope.

It was toward that hope that tens of thousands of Dutch leaned, quitting their war-devastated homeland. They came first from the agricultural sector, but by the mid-1950s, skilled workers and professionals were arriving in large numbers. Ontario was still the most popular destination, followed by Alberta, British Columbia and the Maritimes. By the late 1960s, an estimated 150,000

Dutch immigrants had arrived. Today over 358,000 Dutch and their descendants make Canada home, and comprise the tenth largest ethnic group in the country.

Overcoming Obstacles

When Jane and Bob Aberson settled in Dauphin, Manitoba, they soon realized that making a living on a small farm was a far cry from the idyllic lifestyle of the immigration posters. What often awaited immigrants was low pay and dirt-poor living conditions. Jane Aberson made a little extra money to supplement the farm income by writing a column for a paper back home, tempering the immigration myth with a dose of fact.

The barren prairie life, short growing season and cold winters took the early Dutch immigrants by surprise. But their community grew, as did the desire to help the continuing flow of immigrants from their homeland. In Winnipeg, an organization was set up to give aid to needy immigrants and provide social and cultural activities for the community. It also established the Queen Wilhelmina Fund to give temporary financial aid to immigrants in distress.

Despite the unexpected hardships, many Dutch established family farms that provided enough financial security for them to return to more familiar lines of work such as bookkeeping, carpentry, masonry and construction.

The physical and social isolation of the Dutch immigrants created new opportunities for entrepreneurs. Travelling grocers capitalized on the immigrants' lack of familiarity with or dislike of Canadian foodstuffs and household goods. Small businessmen established sales routes among the immigrants, hawking imported Dutch cigars, apple spread, cheese, windmill cookies, honey-cake, raisin bread and smoked sausage. Dutch textiles and underwear were coveted items, considered to be better made than those in Canada.

The majority of Dutch immigrants shared a lower-middle- and working-class background. But religion wedged between them. While Dutch Roman Catholics formed the largest single religious entity, they've been outnumbered by the combined population of Dutch Protestant groups, many of which have continued their religious traditions in Canada. The majority of Dutch Canadian Catholics and non-Calvinist Protestants belong to Canadian churches, predominantly Presbyterian or Methodist congregations. The only visible Dutch entity on the Canadian religious scene is the Dutch Calvinist or Reformed tradition. The choice for all of them was between assimilation and traditional practices.

The Calvinist immigrants decided to preserve their faith and organized the Winnipeg Christian Reformed Church in 1908. The Dutch church was more than a religious institution. It offered financial support to its indigent congregations, and its clubs, youth groups, and choral organizations provided social activities. Arriving immigrants found part of their native culture alive in the church and were quick to join. But as Dutch immigrants became more familiar with Canada, their dependence on the church lessened. Many severed their connections with the church as soon as they became integrated into Canadian society.

The Dutch-Canadian Legacy

Jane Aberson has been credited with bringing a lot of hard-working immigrants to Canada. Her bare-bones descriptions of the reality and beauty of Canadian life filled the pages of newspapers and speaking halls throughout Holland earlier in the century. She told the true story, not the sugar-coated portrayal of Canada as the land where money grows on wheat.

The result was considerable. The Dutch are the tenth-largest ethnic group in Canada, with a little help from Jane Aberson. Despite their numbers, the Dutch have maintained a relatively low profile in Canada. They are the invisible immigrants and their invisibility was more a matter of choice than chance. Accommodation, integration and even assimilation have been the desire of most Dutch immigrants and their children. Pragmatism asserted itself in the keeping or discarding of things Dutch. Family loyalty and solidarity among communities was worthy of preserving, however, as were the doctrines and expressions of Dutch Calvinism.

For many immigrants, one of the most important ways of retaining cultural identity is in the use of their native language. But the Dutch largely discarded theirs. Dutch immigrants were encouraged to take lessons in conversational English before leaving Holland. Emigration societies and the Dutch government urged fluency in English and stressed that integration was desirable both economically and socially.

As a result, the Dutch language persists only among first-generation immigrants, those who picked up just enough English to get by but who spoke in their native tongue. Subsequent generations have a consistently decreasing knowledge of and fluency in the Dutch language. The Dutch in Canada have recently expressed interest in reviving their language, one example being the DUCA (the Dutch-Canadian credit union) in Toronto which offers Dutch language instruction to its members and their children.

But other cultural remnants and memories remain. Family names are an important means of identification and the Dutch chose to keep them because they weren't too difficult to pronounce. Dutch businesses are often recognizable by the names of the proprietors—Voortman's Cookies, for example—or by the prominence of the windmill symbol. It is a testament to these immigrants that anything Dutch suggests cleanliness, hard work and quality. It's a reputation that favours financial success.

In recent years, with stimulation from the federal government's multicultural program, Dutch Canadian clubs have developed and become involved in ethnic festivals in Winnipeg, Toronto and Calgary. The Canadian Association of Netherlands Studies has attempted to encourage the study of the Dutch role in the world and participation in Canadian cultural events.

Sources

A Bittersweet Land: The Dutch Experience in Canada, 1890–1980, Herman Ganzevoort. McClelland & Stewart, Toronto, 1988.

The Canadian Encyclopedia, World Edition, McClelland & Stewart, Toronto, 1998.

The Fitzhenry & Whiteside Book of Canadian Facts & Dates, Jay Myers. Fitzhenry & Whiteside, Richmond Hill, 1991.

From the Prairies with Hope, Jane L. Aberson. Canadian Plains Research Centre, University of Regina, Regina, first reprint 1998.

A History of Manitoba, Volume Two: Gateway to the West. Great Plains Publications, Winnipeg, 1994.

Holland of the Dutch, Demetrius C. Boulger. Sir Isaac Pitman & Sons, London, 1913.

Holland of Today, George Wharton Edwards. The Penn Publishing Company, Philadelphia, 1919.

A Hundred Years of Agriculture in Manitoba, 1881–1981, Report by Manitoba Agriculture.

The Magnificent Abersons, directed by Laurence Green. White Pine Pictures, Toronto, 1999.

Acknowledgements

There is almost always a small family behind every true act. Lynn Cunningham is the best damned editor in this country. She blesses me with her friendship and unwavering ability. Thank you.

Researcher Siobhan Roberts has accompanied me on this long journey and has earned my gratitude.

And to my publisher, Kim McArthur, whose fierce and Celtic passion safeguards tenderness. And to the mightiest, merriest publishing team: Sherie, Molly, Ruth and Thea.

There are Norm Bolen, Sydney Suissa and Phyllis Yaffe of History Television, who were the first to offer this idea a home. They have championed *A Scattering of Seeds* for three television seasons and given us all a sense of our worth. As has the dedication of Paul deSilva at Vision and Jacinthe Brisebois at RDI.

There is the White Pine Pictures production team who absolved my absence to write this book and kept other dreams alive: my partner Peter Raymont, and Maria, Diana, Margaret, Pat and Lynda. Thank you.

Finally, there are the Canadian filmmakers who first brought these stories to our television series, *A Scattering of Seeds*. These are filmmakers who refused amnesia and dug through archives and memories to make beautiful films and moving tributes. They are Peter d'Entremont, Sylvia Sweeney, Juliann Blackmore, Keith Lock, David Adkin, David Paperny, Ali Kazimi and Laurence Greene.

These are Canadian stories by Canadian filmmakers. Please support our work with your interest.

Image Credits

p. xx Painting of Philippe d'Entremont courtesy of Pere Maurice LeBlanc.

p. 24 Painting of Father Bernard McGauran courtesy of the Musée du Québec.

p. 56 Mary Ann Shadd courtesy of the North Buxton Museum and Historic Site.

p. 82 T. Phillips Thompson courtesy of the National Archives of Canada.

p. 112 Sigursteinn and Stephanie Oddson courtesy of Carol Robertson.

p. 134 Lem Wong courtesy of the Wong Family.

p. 158 Martha Purdy Black courtesy of Florence Whyard.

p. 192 Morris Schumiatcher courtesy of David Paperny; Chaisa and Judah courtesy of the Schumiatcher family.

p. 218 Bagga Singh courtesy of the Singh family.

p. 240 Bob and Jane Aberson courtesy of the Aberson family.

A Scattering of Seeds, as seen on HISTORY TELEVISION

1/Something from Nothing: The Shumiatcher Saga

The first film of the series profiles the legendary Shumiatcher family of Calgary.

2/The Force of Hope: The Legacy of Father McGauran

The heroic efforts of an Irish priest to comfort thousands of dying immigrants.

3/The Road Chosen: The Story of Lem Wong

We follow Lem Wong, who laboured in Chinese laundries from Vancouver to Cape Breton.

4/ For the Love of God: The Mennonites and Benjamin Eby

The story of Benjamin Eby and the history of the Mennonite community of St. Jacob's, Ontario.

5/ Breaking the Ice: The Story of Mary Ann Shadd

The spotlight falls on black woman Mary Ann Shadd, abolitionist, integrationist, and teacher.

6/ Acadian Spirit: The Legacy of Philippe d'Entremont

Peter d'Entremont explores his own ancestry in the Acadian community of Pubnico, Nova Scotia.

7/ Sons and Daughters: The Italians of Schreiber

We follow the progress of a whole village as they move from Calabria, Italy, to work on the CPR in the town of Schreiber, Ontario.

8/ Watari Dori: A Bird of Passage

This is the story of Irene Tsuyuki, a Japanese-Canadian who was interned in the B.C. interior during the Second World War and returned to Canada as an immigrant.

9/ The Impossible Home: Robert Kroetsch and his German Roots

German prairie roots are explored as novelist and poet Robert Kroetsch is profiled.

10/ Passage from India

Bagga Singh journeys from a remote farming village in the Punjab to work in the sawmills of B.C.

11/ The Fullness of Time: Ukrainian Stories from Alberta

We trace the history of the Spak family from the first Ukrainian settlement in Alberta to grandson writer/filmmaker Harvey Spak.

12/ The First Seeding

The legacy of Louis Hébert, the first farmer to sow wheat in Quebec.

13/ A Land as Green as the Sea

A family comes from Scotland to Alberta and goes on to found a Pulitzer Prize-winning newspaper in Edmonton.

14/ First Lady of the Yukon: Martha Black
American Adventurer Martha Black heads to the Yukon gold rush and becomes the first woman Member of Parliament from the Yukon.

15/ An English Sense of Justice: T. Phillips Thompson
T. Phillips Thompson, grandfather of Pierre Berton, is a Toronto newspaperman and champion of the poor and working class.

16/ Brothers from Vietnam: The Story of the Lais and the Bessais
Carl Bessai's personal account of sponsoring a Vietnamese "boat" family and their relationship over the years.

17/ New Norway: The Immigrant Trail
The legacy of three generations of a Norwegian family who emigrated to Alberta in 1912.

18/ Straight Arrow: The Janusz Zurakowski Story
The story of Janusz Zurakowski, a Polish aviator who became an Avro Arrow test pilot.

19/ The Magnificent Abersons
Jane Aberson's letters home became a "how to" column for other Dutch emigrants.

20/ Voice of Freedom
Ugandan refugee Opiyo Oloya became an important part of Toronto's African culture through his community radio program.

21/ Saga of Hope: An Icelandic Odyssey
Two Icelandic families are followed as their fortunes are made and broken in rural Manitoba in the early 1900s.

22/ The Stowaway
A profile of Antonio de Silva, a Portuguese stowaway who arrived in Newfoundland in 1920, and went on to open a boarding house that became home away from home for the famous White Fleet.

23/ Opening Night
George Farhood, a Lebanese immigrant to Montreal in 1889, and his son, opened one of Quebec's first francophone theatres.

24/ The Wanderer: The Story of Reverend Sang-Chul Lee
Korean immigrant Sang-Chul Lee settled in Toronto in the 1960s and became the moderator of Canada's United Church.

25/ The Boatswain: Poet and Writer Radovan Gajic
Recently arrived Serbian poet, Radovan Gajic, is the caretaker and community leader of a high-rise apartment building in Toronto.

26/ The Haitian Heart of Love
Haitian Jesuit Karl Lévêque arrived in Montreal in the 1970s. He used sport, religion and community radio to rally his community and to build bridges into Quebec society.

This book was set in Palatino
with a vertical compression of 90%,
at Moons of Jupiter, Toronto